One Man's Morecambe Bay

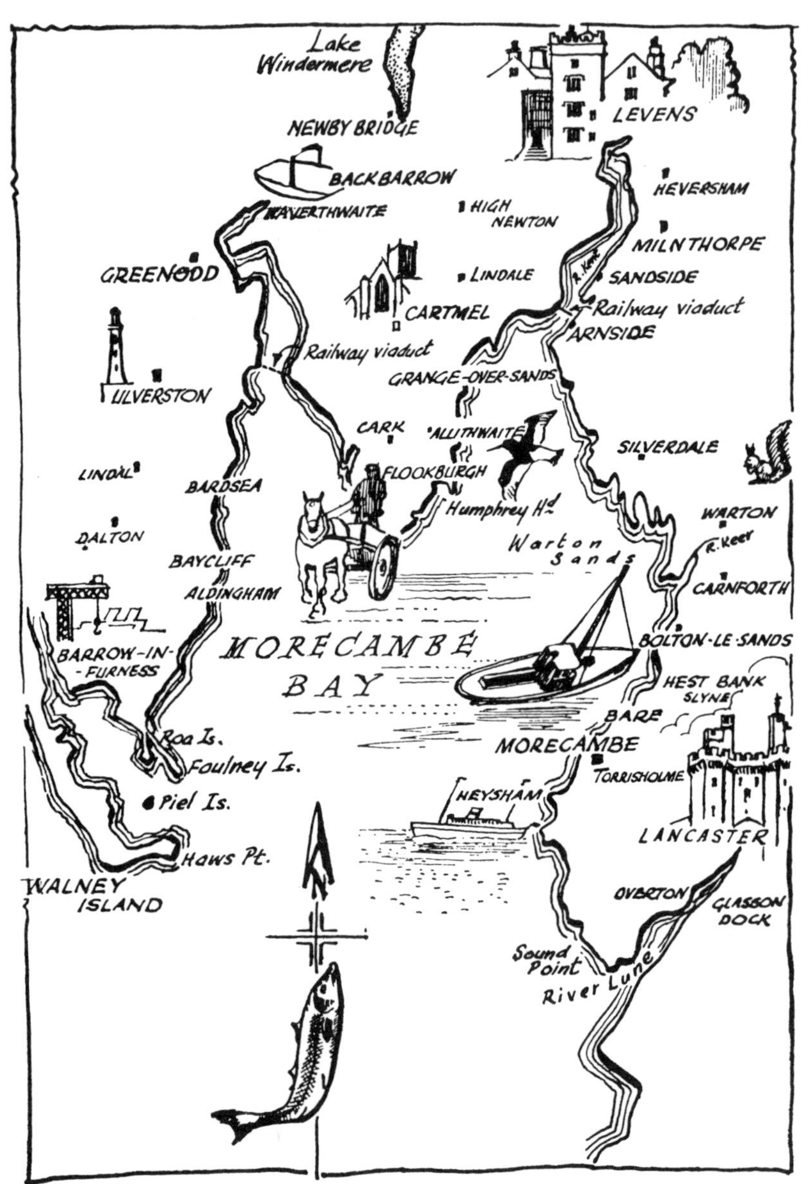

Lake Windermere
NEWBY BRIDGE
BACKBARROW
HAVERTHWAITE
GREENODD
ULVERSTON
LINDAL
DALTON
BARDSEA
BAYCLIFF
ALDINGHAM
BARROW-IN-FURNESS
Roa Is.
Foulney Is.
Piel Is.
Haws Pt.
WALNEY ISLAND
Railway viaduct
CARTMEL
CARK
FLOOKBURGH
HIGH NEWTON
LINDALE
GRANGE-OVER-SANDS
ALLITHWAITE
Humphrey Hd.
LEVENS
HEVERSHAM
MILNTHORPE
SANDSIDE
R. Kent
Railway viaduct
ARNSIDE
SILVERDALE
WARTON
R. Keer
Warton Sands
CARNFORTH
BOLTON-LE-SANDS
HEST BANK
SLYNE
BARE
MORECAMBE
HEYSHAM
Torrisholme
MORECAMBE BAY
LANCASTER
OVERTON
GLASSON DOCK
Sound Point
River Lune

One Man's Morecambe Bay

by
Cedric Robinson
Guide to the Sands

Dalesman Books
1984

The Dalesman Publishing Company Ltd.,
Clapham, via Lancaster, LA2 8EB
First published 1984
© Cedric Robinson, 1984.

ISBN: 0 85206 808 5

I dedicate this book to all who have worked the bay for their livelihood in the past, and those who continue to do so.

Printed in Great Britain by Fretwell & Brian Ltd.,
Healey Works, Goulbourne Street, Keighley, West Yorkshire.

CONTENTS

Cover photograph of Roa Island, Morecambe Bay, by S. C. Sedgwick.
Line drawings by Olive Robinson.
Map by E. Gower.

Acknowledgements

My thanks must go out to the following who contributed towards this publication. Without the kindness and co-operation of these people, it would not have been possible.
S. Baxter; Bob Benson; H. Bradley; J. Braid; Mrs. P. Braithwaite; T. Butler; Peter Cherry; Mr. & Mrs. D. Cooper; J. Duerdon; Mr. Edmondson, Morecambe; Lynda Halhead; Mrs. M. Holms; B. Jackson; S. Long; S. Moore; D. L. Mosey, The Visitor, Morecambe; E. Nicholson; B. Norris; Mr. Rooksby, Cumbria Trust for Nature Conservation, South Walney Reserve; J. Shaw; Mrs. E. Tyson; Mrs. Wild, North Scale, Walney; Mrs. E. R. Williams; John Wilson, Leighton Moss Nature Reserve.
I wish also to thank most sincerely my wife Olive for the help she gave me in my research, and for finding the time to illustrate the text.

Cedric Robinson, with daughter Jean, fishing well down in the Bay for white flukes.
(Manchester Daily Mail)

Foreword

SINCE I was appointed Guide to the Sands in 1963, the walks across Morecambe Bay have become more popular with each season and are known to thousands of people throughout the British Isles and overseas too. No doubt the publication of several booklets about the bay and its flora and fauna, including one by W. R. Mitchell, *Across Morecambe Bay,* along with my own book *Sand Pilot of Morecambe Bay* and radio broadcasts and television appearances I have made, have certainly widened the horizons of a great many people. Many of them would never have taken part in this unique experience if it had not been for the publicity brought to them in this way. Seasons vary according to time and tides and, although all suitable dates are chosen by the Guide for the period of the walks, which is from early May to mid September, there is no shortage of people who want to take part.

As the Guide to the Sands, I get many requests from various organisations, schools and other groups, both locally and far afield, to give talks about the bay and my lifetime's experiences on and around this most interesting area. Times have changed, and people have more leisure on their hands, but nowadays being the Guide during the season is a very busy and strenuous occupation, and I have in the last few years become well-known to thousands of people.

This book has been written in response to this interest. It concentrates on the fisherfolk of Morecambe Bay, but also looks at the history and wildlife of an area extending from Knott End to Walney Island — as well as, of course, at the walk itself. In many ways there is nowhere else in the world that can equal the Bay, and especially one of its sunsets. With the tide out, the colours are reflected from the wet sand and narrow channels of water, a blaze of red and yellow against the blue-grey of Black Coombe.

1. Shifting Sands

MORECAMBE BAY, the big crooked bay, as its name signifies, has on its northern shore the Cartmel and Furness areas. The hills of the Lake District have for hundreds of years formed a barrier hard to overpass but which also help to shelter the Cartmel peninsula from the harsh northern weather. This peninsula is divided from the Lancashire side of the bay by the well known Lancaster Sands, called quick or living sands. In truth these miles of sand which are left bare at low tide are the beds of four rivers which wander out into this vast yellow plain and form new channels for themselves everyday. Where the water lies on the surface, the sand is firm beneath and there is little danger; but where, as often happens following high tides and heavy rainfall, there is the great danger as the water works its way below unseen. Yet, travellers made their way across the sands from Lancaster to Ulverston and beyond as this was the principal route of communication for the people living on the southern and northern shores of Morecambe Bay before the coming of the railway and other modern forms of transport.

Crossing the sands was a dangerous and a difficult operation, but this did not deter the many who used the route regularly. Looking through the Cartmel Parish registers shows that the sands were widely used for passenger traffic, through the recordings of the many who lost their lives. Most of the registers of the old parish churches bordering the bay contain many entries of such people who were drowned while attempting the crossing of the treacherous sands. From the late sixteenth century until 1880 such burial entries numbered no less than 141 in the registers of Cartmel Priory Church. All these entries tell us nothing more than that death was due to drowning while out on the sands. Before the appointment of the official Guide to the Sands, people ran great risks as they would even today if they attempted the passage alone.

Pilling Sands on a pleasant May evening looked the ideal place for five youths to put their motor bikes through their paces as they had done several times before. They saw no danger. They had a wonderful time in the space and freedom of the sands, until one lad, trying to cross a muddy gully, was thrown from his machine and both boy and bike were soon engulfed in the infamous quicksands. The more the lad struggled to free himself, the deeper he sank. His pals tried frantically to extricate him but only found they too were sinking. Managing to get free, they spent a further precious hour scooping away the sand with their bare hands but to no avail. One of the lads

Drama off Silverdale — a boy is rescued from Morecambe Bay's treacherous quick-sands. (Lancashire Evening Post).

decided to go for help and called the police. The village bobby was first on the scene and by now it was beginning to get dark, but even at this time they did not see the danger they were all in. Eventually the policeman called the Fire Brigade. Later still, Liverpool MRSC were informed and despatched Knott End Coastguard Auxiliaries who are well versed in such incidents. A lifeboat and a helicopter were also alerted but it was too late, the flooding tide ran in up the gully at terrific speed and the sea and the dreaded quicksands had claimed another victim.

His heavy motoring boots and his struggling had made his plight worse. If, instead of using up precious time in attempting to rescue their pal themselves, the youths had called the Coastguards NOT the police, his life could have been saved. The Coastguards are fully equipped with all the knowledge and implements necessary for rescue, and anyone seeing people in difficulties out on the sands should always get to a telephone and dial 999 and ask for COASTGUARDS first as they are the people who can give the

A period view of Grange from the sands, looking towards the then new Clare House Pier built in 1893. Notice the absence of a promenade.

best assistance. They will alert other services if they need assistance.

On the turn of the tide, it took fifteen firemen, ambulance men and police to free the lad's body. The doctor who held a post mortem said death was due to asphyxia — drowning. The four fractured ribs and other superficial injuries were caused after death, by ropes used to release the body of the youth.

Within three days of the Pilling tragedy there was another drama in the quicksands, this time at Silverdale. Luckily the tide was ebbing, and the Liverpool MRSC were called immediately. Arnside auxiliaries were alerted and were on the scene with their mud-sledge, duck boards and other life-saving equipment in quick time. The team from Arnside are exceedingly efficient, and John Duerden and his men have taken part in many rescues from the quicksands of Morecambe bay. They have the best local knowledge of this beautiful but treacherous bay. In this case as usual they set to work with a will, and after much hard work extricated the boy, who in spite of the intense cold and the fact he was an asthmatic, helped his rescuers by keeping calm under circumstances where a thirteen year old may well have panicked.

As the water is driven out of the sand around the victim, it becomes like a cement casing, and any pressure only hardens it further and movement becomes impossible. Arnside auxiliaries have some very specialised equipment, and a few years ago gave a demonstration of their mud-sledge, something like a wide flat-bottomed boat, which, because of its shape and size, lies on top of the mud, enabling the men to get close to the victim without getting into mud themselves.

On 16 April 1982 two families were trapped out a hundred yards or so from the shore near to Sandside on the sands they knew so well. They were enjoying the evening walk when suddenly the younger girl found herself sinking in the mud. In no time at all they were all trapped in the dreaded quicksands. After a struggle the youngsters managed to get free but the others, weighted down with heavy clothing and wellingtons, sank deeper as they tried to release themselves. A rescuer also became trapped but with the plank he was bringing to help the others, he managed to get free and with other help rescued the rest of the group. The Coastguard, John Duerden of Arnside, warned people, particularly holidaymakers, NOT to go out on the sands unless they had exceptional knowledge of tides and sands.

It was 1501 before the first guide held office at Grange over Sands as "Carter upon Kent Sands", he being paid by the Prior of Cartmel, and it was not until dissolution of the monasteries that guides were appointed by the Duchy of Lancaster. Travellers crossing the sands before that date would possibly have been given help and advice from the local fisherfolk out in the bay, but people did still lose their lives while making the crossing, and this is no doubt why the post of guide was created. Until that time the coach drivers had to choose their own routes across the bay.

Coaches, in the early days, carried as many as thirteen passengers inside and others on the top, plus luggage, but as many accidents occurred with these top-heavy vehicles, and lives too were lost, it was decided to make the coaches much lighter and to carry fewer passengers. In this way, the quicksands were cheated of many of their victims.

The coach route started from a little inn at Lancaster, with a drive of three miles or so before reaching the shore at Hest Bank. The larger stage coaches swayed from side to side, wending their way across the long stretch of sand, sometimes overladen, and with the many types of sand encountered on the route, much pressure was put on horses and driver, even before they plunged into the deep channel, but after much whipping and splashing of the horses, they were soon out of the water and safely on the sands again at the other side. Depending on the conditions and the state of the tide at the time, the guide would previously have crossed the river on horseback, then, on meeting the coach, he would ride on well ahead avoiding the dangerous gulleys, dykes and quicksands and warning the driver if any of the quicksands had shifted or become unsafe since he had marked out the route beforehand with small branches of laurel. These markers are called brobs, and they are still used when marking the routes even today. The guide, after seeing the coach safely over the most dangerous places, would suddenly appear at the window of the coach, and hold out his old cap and ask recognition of his services. He would then ride off satisfied and would meet and conduct other travellers across the bay.

Although the bay had a reputation of being dangerous, with ordinary precautions and consultation with the guide, the journey from Hest Bank to Kents Bank and Grange over Sands, or across the Ulverston estuary in fine weather, could be as safe as it was enjoyable. The fact is that most of the accidents on record have taken place as the result of carelessness, or plain disobedience to the advice of the guides. Although the stage coach ran regularly between Lancaster and Ulverston across the sands of Morecambe Bay, it was discontinued at one time, as the proprietors of the coaches found the sands becoming increasingly dangerous, but they were running again as soon as the sands had hardened up to make a safe route.

Cart Lane and Carter Road, Kents Bank, Grange over Sands, have been associated with fishermen and Guides over the Sands for centuries, most noticeably in the eighteenth century. When the Guide whom Henry VIII appointed, Thomas Hogeson, died, the office of Guide was thrown open and someone of the name of Carter took over, and for some centuries the office remained with this family. While looking through the Cartmel Priory registers, I found one Richard Carter was buried there, and also other members of the Carter family. George Carter, who was baptised at Cartmel, was the son of John Carter, who is described in the register as "Ye Guide to the Sands", in the year 1716. Though this is the final mention of his office, it is reasonable to believe that other Carters of Cart Lane were also "Guides to the Sands". In the eighteenth century, the word "Carter" was in use instead of the title "Guide". and the house where the Guide to the Sands now lives, was called "Carter House". It would seem too that Carter Road was so named because it led down to the Carter's house, and Cart Lane was the lane where the carts and horses went on their way to the sands.

The coming of the Furness Railway around the shores of the bay in 1857 almost put an end to the sands crossings overnight and although Guides were still appointed, there were times when the sands were desolate, apart from the fisherfolk who had to make their living from them. In those times Guide's Farm had much more land than it has today. There was land at Lindal, Grange and Allithwaite which belonged to the farm, and very few of the earlier guides were full-time fishermen. They combined farming with their duties of Guide and made a living that way.

In 1867 a connection by marriage of the Carter family was appointed to the office of Guide to the Sands. Unfortunately, he was too fond of the bottle and drank to excess. His conduct led to an enquiry at Grange over Sands in 1873. John Fell held the enquiry, and the town clerk of Morecambe, Mr. William Tilly, defended the Guide. He was found guilty and was removed

Another view of Grange before the building of the promenade, this time from Blawith Point. On the right is the Furness Railway.

from office. Mr. George Sedgwick was appointed in his place, and served from 1873 until his death in the autumn of 1918.

In the spring of 1919, Mr. J. Burrows was appointed Guide to the Sands, after serving in H.M. Forces for four years, when he took part in many of the battles in France. He was badly wounded in the leg. After a year in hospital, he was discharged and took over the office of Guide to the Sands, at Cart Lane, and his pre-war occupation of fisherman.

For several years the sea continually washed the marsh at the Silverdale and Hest Bank side of the bay. With my knowledge of the bay, I am finding similar happenings today in much the same areas and I believe that these happenings work in cycles in Morecambe Bay. There are of course changes occurring each and every day, with each tide, but these drastic ones seem to be in cycles of a century. Even today, on the foreshore at Silverdale, one can see a slightly higher embankment of the original marshland, which is a reminder of all those years ago, when the river Kent ran so close to the shore on that side of the bay that it was a hazard to the sheep which were used to a much greater area of marshland to graze on. They would gad about in the hottest weather and many would attempt to cross the river and were swept away out to sea. The guides too would no doubt have had great difficulty in finding safe routes, as the river formed a perilous barrier, particularly in wet and cold weather and when mist and fog envelope the bleak, open plains of the sands of Morecambe Bay. Fog and mist come down so suddenly out there and lives are put in jeopardy, sometimes lost in these circumstances miles from anywhere.

In the year 1828 John Briggs wrote that he had got a good deal of information out of the old Carter who explained to him the manner in which the flukes and cockles were caught on the sands. The old man told him that the people employed in the occupation were generally selected from the blackguards (lowest classes). He also told of someone who, having heard that the Guide was giving up his job, was keen to take over the office. He said to the Guide, "I think your business must be a dangerous one. Are the guides never lost out there on the sands?" "I nivver knew anyone lost," replied the sly old Carter, "But there are yan or two drowned now and again, but we generally find 'em, I don't remember anyone being lost, except just yan and he was a true hero." Two gentlemen came to the Carter one very wild night, and asked to be guided across. Saying it was madness to attempt the sands crossing that night, he refused to go with them. The travellers however insisted, saying it was a matter of life and death. "Nay," said the old Carter, "It's likely there'll be may-er than yan death if tha tries to cross tan-neet." But the men were determined and set off out onto the sands alone. "Well," the Carter reasoned, "I knows't place better than they do, so I'd better go an help 'em." He mounted his horse, followed them and led them over the dangerous areas of the bay. On returning, he was himself overtaken by the incoming tide. His horse came back alone, and that was all that was ever seen of the Guide who was faithful unto death.

There has been from time immemorial, a smaller over-sands route at Sandside, where the Kent estuary is about a mile across, on which the inhabitants of Storth were dependent for their supply of fuel from Foulshaw Mosses. The peat-carts were coming across, late one summer afternoon as a thunderstorm was growling itself away over the distant mountains, the inky black clouds contrasting weirdly with the pale limestone of Whitbarrow, whilst nearer at hand the sun gleamed on long sandbanks and rippling channels. The carts approached along the opposite bank, then descended into the river-bed. Where water was met, the horses threw up a glittering shower at every step. The sand was very firm, no route was apparently sought for, as the tide was at farthest ebb, and the river almost dry after a prolonged drought. Under less favourable conditions, precautions would have been taken. But even at this short, shallow ford, narrow escapes have been recorded and occasional fatalities.

Some years ago, a man left the Foulshaw Farms as soon as the ebb allowed, to bring a couple of loads of slate from the Arnside district. He had reckoned to be back at Sandside early enough to cross before the tide again rose, but when he reached the inn by the shore, a grey strip of sea-water was already forcing its way up the river. Though he fully realised the danger, he determined to make an attempt, and whipped up the horses accordingly. At that time, the two rivers were making their way to the sea by separate channels, one close to either bank. The Bela was negotiated without difficulty, then came a long stretch of sands to the Kent channel, which was backwatering in an alarming manner. There was now no retreat, so the man drove his horses into the choppy, broken water as quickly as possible. Down they went into the groove of the channel, the water rising under the horses. Wave after wave struck the convoy, but the heavily laden carts were not easily overturned. Just as the centre was reached though, a mammoth breaker struck the last cart which overturned. At imminent peril to himself the driver made his way through the surge, now almost up to his neck, to the unfortunate horse, which was rapidly suffocating. It was a matter of urgency to cut the harness, and the writhing horse did not make things any easier. However, in a few seconds all was severed, and the horse struggled to his feet again. The other horse and cart were by this time safe on the far bank. No lives were lost but as the tide receded, the farm hands went to look for the cart and its load. The former had been carried some two hundred yards upstream by the strong current. Of the slates, only a few were lying embedded in the sand, the rest were never recovered.

2.   Cross-Bay Walks

A SERIES of articles in the "Morecambe Visitor" first created an interest in the cross bay walks, the excellent fishing and other pursuits. These articles were later published in book form, and the first edition came out in 1936, followed by other editions in 1937 and 1938. In the days before this little book was published, few people had heard of the walks across the sands and only a very few had made the crossing on foot. During the summer months of 1937, more people crossed the sands from Hest Bank to the Guides House at Cart Lane than in any other year during the last half century. This was primarily due to that little book, *The Sands of Morecambe Bay,* and was also helped by a radio broadcast given by Mr. Jack Burrows, the guide at that time. During the war years, 1939 to 1945, there were no crossings of the sands, from Hest Bank to Kents Bank.

A Mr. Leonard Smith sent me a very nice letter after reading my book, *Sand Pilot of Morecambe Bay.* He was very interested in the book as he had lived in Morecambe and Heysham from 1941 to 1949, and the chapter "Crossing the Bay on Foot" appealed to him, as he told me he was quite proud to have been a member of a party on a crossing of the Bay on Saturday, 14 June 1947. It was quite an occasion as the party was seen off from Hest Bank by a crowd of people, including the Mayor of Morecambe, Mr. Willacy, and the well-known radio and television personality, Wilfred Pickles, who was appearing in Morecambe at the time. This was to be the first organised crossing of the sands since the war. I believe one or two small parties had crossed previously, but had just started out on their own. Leonard Smith said he managed a chat with Wilfred Pickles, and can recall him saying, "Well, I've seen some silly beggers in my time, but none so daft as you lot!" They started off from Hest Bank at noon and reached Kents Bank at 3.30 p.m. It was rather a dull day but the crossing was good. The only excitement was the water up to their knees and thighs in the Kent Channel. They were met at the river by the young guide, Mr. Jack Burrows junior, along with his uncle Mr. T. Wilkinson and an assistant with a boat. Mr. Smith thought the party was a relatively small one, and he has a couple of photographs of this particular event. He says it is an experience he will always remember. He was forty-four years old at the time, and now at seventy-nine years of age he feels he could tackle the walk once again.

A bay like ours is always an attraction, and hundreds of walkers are now lured into taking part on the guided walks I organise each year. There is such a sense of freedom and adventure when you stride across the wide expanse of sand with only the sound of the surf and the cries of the gulls for company, except for the conversation of the walkers, which is going on all the time throughout the walk.

I often wonder how many of the walkers realise just what preparation goes into the finding of a safe route to make this a carefree and enjoyable occasion. Conditions at the time of the walk play a big part in making it a memorable one. However, seasons do vary and some years rainfall is well above the average, making conditions at times rather unpleasant.

The spring of 1983 was the wettest on record, and with the long winter of high tides, backed by gale force winds, there were bound to be changes in the course of the Kent and Keer. On May 6th, my son-in-law Chris and I were to plan a walk which was to take place on the following day, and a second one on the next day after that. At 9.50 in the morning we took the train from Grange-over-Sands to Carnforth. As I am not a regular contributor to British Rail, it is interesting to see just what the charges will be, and the difference from one year to the next. Chris paid at the ticket office and I heard the clerk say, "One pound sixty, sir." I thought to myself that isn't too bad for the two of us. It cost me almost as much as that just for myself last season.

There were plenty of vacant seats as the train pulled into the station. We sat down and as the train started we had a good view of the estuary and the river Kent as it flowed, with force, through the arches of the viaduct. I could see right away that our trek across the sands was going to be a bad one, and that we were going to be lucky, very lucky, if we found a place in the river shallow enough to cross.

We left the train at Carnforth and were just in time to catch a bus to Bolton-le-Sands, which was waiting for the train to disgorge its passengers. Our walk across the bay was to start at 10.15 a.m., so we took a walk around Hest Bank and then a stroll along the shore, before setting out. I cut some brobs — small branches from the hedgerow — with my knife. I thought they would be useful as markers on the route we were about to take across the Keer and the Kent channel, and for any other feature which I thought ought to be kept in mind. We were suitably clad for whatever weather we should find out in the bay, as it is so changeable — extra jersey, waterproof, etc., and we also had a flask of hot coffee with us.

It had rained all the previous day, and although it was fine now, for the time being, visibility was poor, with hazy conditions and very humid. All landmarks were blotted out from view. It was now four hours after high water — and time for us to make a move. The sun was trying to break through the haze and I could just make out the rocky outcrops of Priest Skeer. As we came up to the Skeers, we changed our direction, and walked on towards the river Keer, which runs out from Carnforth into the bay.

There was not a breath of wind; the only sounds, the electric trains on the main line, coming from the land, and the thrilling calling of the waders, of which there are about seventeen species in Morecambe Bay. These sounds could be used as a guide to one's position. Keeping the sound on my right, I knew that I was moving in the correct direction. Although it was still hazy, I could see, vaguely, the outline of the shore in the distance. I knew in my mind that dramatic changes had taken place since I had been over this area a short time ago.

Many walkers who have crossed the sands under my guidance will have noticed that at one stage of the walk a car had been engulfed in quicksands but was just visible, so that I was able to use it as a marker. Car Dyke — as I had nicknamed it — was normally a freshwater dyke owing to drainage from the land. What changes had taken place! Terribly big bracks, yards high and soft to cross in places. We could make little headway and had to keep close in to the shore. What a hair-raising experience, as huge chunks of sand, making the noise of cannon fire, toppled into the dyke bottom after being undermined by the flowing current of the recent heavy rains. I was beginning to wonder what surprises there were in store for us on reaching the river Keer. Visibility was still a matter of yards and the whole situation was becoming very eerie. In these conditions, out in the bay, things occur suddenly. A dyke appears as if from nowhere, and one has to be on the look-out all the time. It would be very easy to lose one's bearings. I have never seen conditions so bad as this and I hope that I shall not see them again. Conditions were the worst I have seen in my whole lifetime.

The Kent channel has eaten its way over towards the Silverdale-Carnforth and Bolton-le-Sands side of the bay, and has got a hold on the Silverdale marshes. The winter months of 1982-3, with high tides and north-westerly gales which caused havoc around our coasts, played a great part in drawing up these changes, and now, with the outlet of the river Keer being such a short distance from the land, this limits the area on which a party can cross in safety. I looked over the limited space left to us, and then started to cross, using my staff to prod the dangerous quicksands. I shouted to Chris to follow, but not to step in my tracks or he would go down — it was terrible. The sand was moving all around us, and although we both made it to the other side, safely, I can honestly say that I was thankful when our feet touched firm ground.

It was easy now for me to make a decision on the future walks, as it is just impossible for any party to cross the river Keer in safety. The slag-heaps at Carnforth are only a stone's throw away from where we stood, and as I walked over now to the brack edge of the river Kent, one could see what the

A quiet evening on the upper reaches of Morecambe Bay at Arnside. Fording the Kent down-river from this point can often cause major problems for cross-Bay walkers. (T. Parker)

strength of the tides can do. Looking up the bay towards Silverdale, the height of the bracks must have been at least ten to twelve feet, dropping away sometimes, after being weakened by the outgoing tide. These extremes of the movement of the river only occur in cycles of seventy to one hundred years.

I now knew that future walks could not start from Morecambe Lodge, as they have done in the past. I now had to see what awaited us further up in the bay at Jenny Brown's Point, and out from Silverdale. I already knew that only in the last week, a few days before the original crossings were to take place, the river Kent, well up in the bay, between Arnside and Silverdale, had suddenly moved from the Grange side, where it had been all winter, over to the Silverdale side, running close in to the rocks at Park Point, below Arnside Knott and following the old river bed, or lyring as it is known locally, which was left six years ago.

Now we were on the move again, taking notice of all the changes. At Jenny Brown's Point we sat down for a short break and had a drink from our flask which was most welcome. The trek over the Carnforth marsh was a long one, owing to the Kent channel drawing all the drain-offs from the land into deep gullies. This is what happens when a river moves in towards the land.

It had taken us two hours to get as far as this — longer than it does when leading a large party. I noticed that the river Kent was running closer at this point than the previous year, but the sands were much the same, although there were a few rocks to contend with. They were as nothing compared with the ordeal of finding our way over the Carnforth marsh. The day had now improved and we could see clearly across the bay to Grange-over-Sands.

I had to look carefully over this huge area and particularly towards Silverdale, near to where the stone skeer is showing above the sands, as the following day a party of school children were to undertake the second half of the walk from Silverdale to Grange-over-Sands. I was not at all pleased with what I found. The sand was neither firm nor soft — and whereas the two of us had walked over the area without difficulty, a larger group would have puddled it up. It was able to bear weight, but seemed full of water and puddly.

From this point the river Kent crossing was only a matter of minutes away, and as we approached it I could tell by the flow of the river that there was a lot of fresh water coming down, and although we followed down the edge until we came across what should have been the best place to cross, the current was so swift, and running so deep, that it was impossible to get through to the other side.

Disappointed, as we edged our way slowly, into the flow of the river, I remembered the words of the TV documentary, "Ready to give — but equally ready to take," and thought of those who had booked their walk well ahead. But these conditions do prevail from time to time, and there is very little one can do about it. I can honestly say that in all the years of leading groups across the bay, cancellations have been very few.

Now, we had to get back to Grange-over-Sands — there was nothing else left for us to do, but it wasn't to be over the sands. Not this day. So taking it all in our stride, we decided to make for Arnside rather than Silverdale. We kept as close to the river as possible and finally we reached Arnside promenade at three in the afternoon, after walking for about five hours. The village was very busy and by this time the weather had vastly improved. The sun was shining as we walked the full length of the promenade. We saw a train crossing the viaduct, making its way towards Grange, and decided as we had missed that one, there would be time for a drink of tea in a nearby cafe. We both felt ready for this by now and the next train was not due until 4.33, so we had quite a long wait.

A rather disappointing day really, although there was nothing anyone could do to improve conditions out in the bay, only to hope for a hot, dry summer to help the shorter version of the walk to be an enjoyable one for everyone concerned.

There is no doubt that the cross bay walks have increased in popularity over the years. The bay has become a magnet for photographers, journalists, people from radio and the different television companies. To hold the post of Sand Pilot, one needs extensive knowledge of the sands, the rivers, the tides and the weather, but I think the most important of all is being bred into a fishing family as I was.

3. Fishing Families

FROM Rampside at the entrance of the Walney Channel, the coast road turns to the north west and forms low ground to Newbiggin. A little further along the coast lies Aldingham, a village five miles east of Barrow in Furness and four miles south of Ulverston. Legend has it that part of the village close to the church was engulfed by sand and sea. From here the land rises very steeply from the shoreline to the village of Baycliff. Aldingham is well sheltered from the northerly wind, as it is almost overhung by Birkrigg Common. The views from here show the vast expanse of the bay, which one would never get tired of looking at. Bardsea, once spelt Bardsey, is a quaint little village overlooking the bay. The old hall on the west side of the road going out from Ulverston was formerly the residence of the Bardsey family. The village is well sheltered with rocks and woods, and has easy access to the south to a bold shore and a pleasant beach.

Along this stretch of coastline, fishing families have followed the sands for their livelihood for centuries. Sadly, most of the characters I have known have passed away these last few years, but no doubt they were a hardy breed. They had a method of fishing for plaice that no other fishing community ever plied. On these sands, large areas of stony ground are called scars and on these the fishermen would set their nets to catch the plaice.

At one time, all established fishing families had deeds for the area where they fished, and each family would guard their own areas with jealousy. Most of the scars are showing today, but with a bay such as ours, nothing stays the same for any length of time. At times they get covered with sand, maybe for years, and then they show up again in later years. All these scars have names — Pruscoe Scar, Ridding Hawk Scar, Headow's How Scar, Swine Stones Scar, Meetings Scar, and many others. Today, there are very few fishermen carrying on the traditional method of fishing for plaice which their forbears followed. There were many familiar characters along this stretch of coastline and one of them was Old Maggie Coward from the village of Scales. She would be seen with her horse and cart going out onto the sands to set nets for plaice and she also gathered cockles which she took to Barrow in Furness, to her customers. She was a widow, and this was her way of making a living.

There was John Butler, formerly of Flookburgh, known to all the locals as Scound. That nickname stuck to him all his life as he fished the bay. Tommy Butler from Baycliff was a cheery character, and, as he was quite small, got the name of 'Lyle Tommy'. He too followed the sands all his life as his father did before him.

At Hilltop, Baycliff, there is usually a sign outside saying "Fish for Sale", but more noticeable than the sign is the figure of a rather large mermaid in the front garden. There has always been much speculation as to how it came there and many tales are woven round it.

Tom Benson's family have fished and sold their catches of plaice and shrimps at the Ulverston Market for years. Tom's mother used to follow the sands regularly with horse and cart, until all the family grew up. It was a hard life but it was accepted in those days, if a living was to be made.

In 1914 the fishermen from around the bay were given the chance of attending what was named the Hatchery. It was a kind of school and they were each paid £3.00 a week for attending. The school was held on Roa Island, and someone from Liverpool came down to take the classes. They learnt about the tides of the bay, the different types of fish and the sizes the fish would grow to in different periods of time. Biology at sea was the base of the lessons. A few men were chosen from the fishing community around the bay each year, and those who didn't get in one year would get the chance the next. They were there for a fortnight at a time. Annual reports from 1903 published details of who taught at the school and who attended the classes.

There are very few fishermen today who follow the coast road sands, and although the horse and cart has been replaced with the diesel-engined tractor, the few men who do some fishing haven't the same urgency. They can take their time on the job. Even so, accidents do happen, as young Tom Butler from Baycliff described to me. He had just arrived at the shrimping grounds with his tractor and trailer which carried the shrimping nets. The fishermen always pulled well into the water before stopping to unhitch the trailer as this along with dropping the nets and making them ready takes up quite a bit of time, so whilst this is going on the tidewater is ebbing away gradually and unnoticed and then when the fisherman has prepared his nets, etc., his tractor and trailer are usually high and dry on the sand at the side of the water. On this day, as Tommy turned on the seat of his big Nuffield tractor, he leaned over slightly to pull a rope which was attached to the pin which should have released the drawbar and the trailer. The pin should have come out quite easily, but not so, it was stuck tight. His idea now was to release the clutch of the tractor with his foot, and this should have done the trick and slackened the pin, but his foot suddenly slipped off the clutch. The tractor lurched forward, and with the front wheels being slightly turned, over went the tractor in three feet of water trapping Tommy under it. Luckily, for Tommy, his uncle Tom and Albert Edmondson were not too far away, and they were soon on the scene. They managed to right the upturned tractor and get home with Tommy as fast as they could. Tommy's mother was so shocked when she saw him and thought he was dead. His face was blue and his eyes were sticking out like marbles. He had water in his lungs but as

A fisherman's tractor fast disappearing into the Morecambe Bay quicksands. There have been a number of near tragedies when tractors have become stuck in this way. (Yorkshire Television)

they had got him home and then to hospital so quickly his life was saved. Although this was a very nasty accident, it would have been a real tragedy if there had been no other fishermen near at the right moment and Tommy wouldn't have been around to tell me this tale. When Tommy was home again, and getting back on his feet, he and his uncle were talking over the near tragedy when in came Albert Edmondson. They had a good laugh as one always can after the event, when they were telling Tommy's mother that, as they pulled Tommy out of the water, he had great difficulty in breathing. Of course, the first thing the rescuers thought of was to take his false teeth out but after a few tugs, they gave up and decided to get Tommy to hospital as quickly as possible. It wasn't until they were telling Tommy's mother about the teeth that she said: "No wonder you couldn't get 'em out, they're 'is own!"

Weather is of the utmost importance to all the fishermen and trawler men who work the sands and fishing grounds of Morecambe Bay and one learns to take an interest in it from a very early age. It has so great an influence on our lives. I am a great believer in the barometer and always refer to it every morning of my life. There are many sayings and signs of weather changes, which I am sure everyone connected with the bay will know, but they are of interest and no doubt are used to advantage.

Here are just a few of those sayings: "Mackerel sky, not long wet, not long dry." "Red sky in the morning, shepherds' warning. Red sky at night, shepherds' delight." "When the old moon is seen in the new moon's arms, it is sign of rain" — that is when the dim image of the moon continues the circle formed by the bright crescent. Before a storm the seagulls venture inland — "Seagull, seagull, sit on sand. It's never fine weather when you're on land". "Rain before seven am, fine before eleven am". "When the mist is from the sea, then good weather it will be".

Many of these sayings come from those who have lived and worked in the midst of the weather, and have need to study it most, like the fishermen and the farmers. In a vast bay like ours, the fisherman's livelihood is often dependent on the weather. For instance, strong winds will bring the tide in much higher, but also along with such gales come masses of seaweed which is brought up from the open seas and is then deposited on the ebb tide. It gets caught in the fishing nets, sometimes to such an extent that the nets are impossible to fish as they are, as we say, completely webbed up with this horrible weedy stuff and become so heavy that no man could lift the net from the sands on his own.

All this depends on what kind of fishing is being done. A good stiff breeze can at times help the catches of flukes, shrimps and the like, but for white-bait, you need reasonably calm weather as too much wind can break up the shoals of such small fish. Heavy rainfall can make major changes in and near to the rivers which flow out into the bay, and one has to be aware of these changes and be on the lookout for danger, for what was a safe area to cross on one tide, could be a trap for the unwary on the following tide.

The fisherfolk across the bay at Silverdale, Bolton-le-Sands and Morecambe did not have the long distances to travel out to the fishing grounds as those further west and this meant that they had no need for the bigger and stronger horse. Small gallowers were used, and one old fisherman used a donkey and cart. He would leave it standing out there on the sands, with a lantern lit, to show the whereabouts of it. Then he would walk the final stretch. The probability was that there was some water to cross somewhere on the journey and it is a well known fact that donkeys don't really take to water as a horse does. This was the reason for leaving the donkey behind. This donkey had stood faithfully for the fisherman for years.

One night, thick fog came down when they were fishing the nets. There were two men out together — the old man with his donkey and his mate.

They decided to make their way back as quick as possible, leaving the nets only half fished, but as they made their way towards the marsh and the donkey, realising that they should have come upon the animal by this time, it dawned on them that though they were moving in the right direction, they had missed their tracks and had not found the donkey. Calling and calling, but there was no sound from the poor beast, and in the dark and the thick fog, all they could do was to make their way landward. What a dreadful experience! The struggle through the dark and the fog, losing the donkey and the added fear of being cut off by the incoming tide and drowned. With these thoughts in their minds they stumbled on until they reached the shore to make their way home.

There was no sleep for them that night thinking of the poor old donkey, and as soon as the tide had ebbed and day break came they set off to see what had happened to the donkey and the cart. Not very far from the shore, they could just make out something and with feelings of dread, they went on to find the donkey lying dead at the spot where he had been left. He had been faithful to the very end, standing at the place where the old man had put him with the lamp and cart. The tide had crept up and drowned him in the dark of the night. What a terribly sad end for such a faithful animal.

Following the sands to provide a living is a dangerous occupation, and

Two studies of Cedric Robinson and his daughter setting out into the Bay for the cockle beds. It is essential to make a careful study of the weather before such a trip is undertaken. (Manchester Daily Mail)

even with a lifetime's experience one is never too old to learn. There are many hazards to be met out there. The ever-changing tide, the dreaded fog and the quicksands, which can cover very large areas. One gets used to living with these dangers and over the years one tends to get wiser.

One old fisherman from Bolton-le-Sands, who was known to be a loner, used to fish out in the bay for shrimps with a hand net. He would make his way to the shore, regularly during the season, carrying his net over his shoulder with a hamper, which was to hold his catch, slung over his back. About a quarter of a mile from the water, he would reach the channel, where he would push his net along the bottom through the water, catching the shrimps. Returning home, he then boiled and picked them himself taking them around the streets to sell them. He often told how he had one dread. That was to be taken ill whilst out on the sands on his own. And so, he always left a lantern lit in the kitchen window when he left to go out shrimping. It could easily be seen by the neighbours, who made it their job to keep an eye open. If the light was still there in the morning, they would have known that something was wrong.

The inevitable happened. The lamp was seen still alight one morning, and so the neighbours could only think the worst had happened. A couple of local chaps who had knowledge of the sands volunteered to go out in search of him, but could find nothing until the third day. They went over the area they had searched the last couple of days, and there they found the body of the fisherman wrapped around with his net. It is said that the bay never releases a body until the third day by which time it would float to the surface. He was found in the area where he had pushed his net, shrimping, for most of his lifetime.

Almost every home in Bolton-le-Sands, Flookburgh and other coastal villages had at one time one or more large brass shells which were used as door-stops. Many years ago when the artillery came to Morecambe and fired live shells to fixed and moving targets out on the sands, the shells exploded and threw out small bullets the size of marbles. The tops of those shells were made of solid brass, so when the firing ceased and the tide was right, local chaps along with the fishermen went out onto the sands and collected them. The shell cases polished up beautifully and were also used as ornaments. One chap in Bolton-le-Sands had several of them turned on a lathe and mounted in a glass case. A common thing then but not many are to be found in the homes today.

In winter time, when fishing wasn't so good with the wild weather, the fishermen had to find other means of making a living. They used to set what they called fly nets which they made from very fine cotton, with about four inch mesh, and knitted by the fishermen themselves. They were set on willow stakes which were cut from the hedgerows, fairly lightweight ones, worked into the sand. The nets were carried out on the backs of the fishermen, not too far out from the shore, near to the tide "brod" in a zig zag fashion, and they were to catch birds which usually fly along the tide-line and would then get trapped in the nets. In the dusk, the nets were difficult for the birds to see and they were set about six feet high with a large bag to allow the birds to tangle in the mesh. Mostly, the birds caught were the oystercatchers, or as the fishermen called them "sea-a-pies", but curlews, dunlin and occasionally rare birds would be caught. Later, the fishermen would be seen round the village streets, with clusters of dead birds hanging by their necks shouting loudly for customers. Most families bought the birds which were good and tasty but with a little bit of a fishy flavour so they were soaked prior to being cooked. They were always skinned not plucked. The dunlin is not much bigger than a sparrow, and they were also skinned. The soaking was first done in salted water to clean them and then again in fresh water.

The setting of these fly nets is banned today and birds of the bay are protected, so everyone can now watch the wonderful flight of the dunlin, and take pleasure in the flocks of oystercatcher, thrill to the haunting call of the curlew, and the many many varieties of seabirds which find their living on the wide expanse of Morecambe Bay.

Another delicacy, which was only available at certain times of the year when shrimp fishing was in full swing was made from the many small flukes caught with the shrimps. Instead of throwing them back they were brought home, their heads and tails snipped off with a pair of sharp scissors. Without any further cleaning, they were put into a stew-pot with alternate layers of butter and flukes. Then the pot, when filled to the top, was either put into a very slow old-fashioned fireside oven, or the dish was roasted. When ready, this delicacy could be cut up into sections being served like a cake, and was greatly relished by the fishermen and their families.

Listening to the singing of the cockles.

4. Flookburgh — and the flukes

THE tidal waters of Morecambe Bay wash the shore within a mile or so of the village of Flookburgh today, but before the coming of the railway, the tide often reached the village itself, sometimes lashing with the fury of a gale, sometimes flowing quietly, barely reaching the coastline. Whatever the weather, fishing was of the greatest importance to the hardy families who were brought up to the tough life of the inshore fisherman, long years ago. Flookburgh, although having only one main street, that street was the major route through which passed the daily stage coach, when, having crossed the treacherous miles of Morecambe Bay sands, the coach made its way to Ulverston in Furness over the even more treacherous sands of the Leven estuary.

Many harrowing incidents are on record, and one that comes to mind happened in the Christmas holidays in the year 1883. There was a family gathering at nearby Holker Hall, the home of the Duke of Devonshire and the Cavendish family. Lord Richard Cavendish, who had a very vivid recollection of the occasion wrote:

"My father, two brothers and a cousin, Gerald Lascelles and I, were riding on the Leven sands. Four of the group had crossed the stream, Cark Beck, the River A, which comes out onto the sands between Ulverston and Flookburgh close to the railway. My young brother's pony refused to cross, and the others waited for him on the far side. The stream had lately changed course and we were standing on the old bed which was noted for quicksands. My brother called out to us to hurry on, but though we had only delayed a minute or so, it was too late. Two of the horses were already fast and quickly sank up to their necks. Luckily we were close to the shore and within a short time we had any amount of assistance. At first, there seemed to be no real danger, until we saw cousin Gerald, up to his waist in the quicksands, trying to keep the horses' mouths and nostrils free from the sand. Men from a farm close by brought straw, planks and ropes and managed after a tremendous struggle to get the horses out".

Among the many narrow escapes, mention must be made of Major Bigland of Bigland Hall, near Haverthwaite, who, when crossing from Lancaster, alone in his gig on a dusky evening, missed the Cartmel headland entirely, and found himself, most fortunately, landing safely near Conishead Priory, Ulverston.

Although Flookburgh is still only a village with little development over the years, at one time it was the market town and probably the largest in the district, as others like Grange and Cartmel have only increased in population and developed during the last hundred years or so. Still to be seen, hidden away behind a row of small cottages on the left-hand side of Main Street, is part of Eccleston Meadow. It was here according to the

Shrimping with horse and cart from Flookburgh — a fascinating 'action picture' of a now vanished way of life. (J. Dodgson)

parish registers of Lakeland, that in the 16th and 17th centuries the many victims of what at that time was called "The Black Plague" were buried in a mass grave. There was a great loss of life from the dreaded "Visitation" and many families were almost wiped out. Although skirted around with houses and other buildings, part of the Eccleston Meadow has been owned by my parents and has been cultivated as a market garden for a number of years.

Most of the houses in Flookburgh are small, but in the past, with a population of two or three hundred, the village could boast of four public houses or inns as they were called in those far off days. There is The Crown Inn, which is the first inn on entering the village, then the Kings Arms, now no longer a pub but it goes under the name of the "Late Kings Arms". Within striking distance central to the village there is the Hope and Anchor, whilst further along Main Street, almost at the bottom of the very steep hill, Sandgate Hill, where the road leads westwards towards the village of Sandgate, stood "The Galloping Horse". The name would seem appropriate because at that time the drivers of the laden stage coaches would have whipped their teams of horses into the gallop in order to prepare them for the hard pull up the hill and away on out of Flookburgh. The name did not stick very long with this pub. The name was justified but loss of trade led to the name being changed to the Punch Bowl, and later, to the Royak Oak. It became a private residence many years ago. The trials and tribulations were not yet over though, as recently a fire destroyed part of the building. I had the opportunity to see inside since it was rebuilt and was shown a wonderful old fashioned fireplace, which had been hidden away for many years and was discovered during the alterations. It is now, I am sure, regarded as a treasure from the past.

Not many villages of the size of Flookburgh could have had so many public houses in competition with each other, but being a market centre, and holding two annual fairs of three days each, at Midsummer and Michaelmas, there would seemingly have been enough trade for all. These inns have now all been modernised, but in the days of the stage coach they would all have had good stabling for horses. After the gruelling journey over the bay, a change of horses was essential. Drivers and passengers would also have needed a rest after the stress and strain of the crossing. According to the state and time of the tide, the coach might reach Flookburgh in the evening, and rather than tackle the second leg of the journey over the sands, probably in the dark or impossible conditions, they would put up at the inn for the night, the horses would be fed and watered and bedded down, ready for a fresh start on the following day, when the tide permitted.

The lowlands of the village were reclaimed early in the last century, and prior to this, the villagers were always on the alert for the extra high tide which could have meant disaster.

At this time, there were about 150 fishermen in the village of Flookburgh, and although horses and carts were used by some of them, most used boats for fishing the harvest of the bay. As there were no modern methods of transport, prior to the coming of the railway, the cockles and mussels which were gathered by the fishermen were carted across the sands to Hest Bank. There they were sent to Preston by canal boat.

Plaice used to be plentiful in those days in the bay, and were sold for one shilling for a score. That would be five pence for twenty pounds in today's decimal currency. Today plaice is a rarity at our side of the bay, whereas the white fluke is plentiful. Mussels were also there for the taking and were to be found on the hard, stony ground or rocky surfaces which were frequently covered by the tide. Owing to the silting up of the bay, none are brought ashore today from areas where once were masses of good quality mussels. Although mussels were to be found on the rocky slopes of Humphrey Head, and further up the bay at Holme Island, and again at Arnside, the favourite fishing ground for the Flookburgh fishermen with their boats was across the Leven estuary where they fished the scars or skeers (stony ground) for the mussels, near to the Ulverston side of the bay.

Harold Manning, of Flookburgh, as a boy of twelve, when he was known as Harold Butler, helped to gather together the words of the old Flookburgh dialect. Flookburgh — Flokis Brugh (Floki is a Norse personal

Two evocative studies of fishermen in former times. Men would go down to the sands in convoy and then spread out — some to fish their fluke nets, others to go cockling or in search of shrimps. (J. Dodgson)

name). Until the last twenty years or so ago, the fishermen of Flookburgh always used a dialect whilst out on the sands. The dialect was mainly made up of Norwegian words and they are still used by the Icelanders in the fishing trade. Harold Manning joined the Royal Navy in 1939 and was sent as a coastguard to the shores of Iceland. In his letters home he stated that the Icelanders not only understood his home dialect, but that when he went out fishing with them he had no difficulty in understanding the terms they used.

Fishermen in those early days lived rough and had little or no education. Feuds were quite common between adjacent villages. In the early 1900s the hostility between the villages of Cark and Flookburgh was so intense that at times it came to blows, and many a scuffle took place on the bridge over the railway which divides the two villages. No other villages around could have housed such different breeds of men. The feuding has died away with the passing of time however, and the younger members of the villages travel around the country, which makes for a better understanding than the narrow life lived in the old days.

The fishermen used to be away from home for many long hours, going out on the ebb tide and returning on the flood or incoming tide. Weather could change quickly and without warning. There were no radio forecasts to tell when a gale could be expected. Fishermen had to depend on their own knowledge, and a freak storm could catch them unawares sometimes with disastrous results.

In 1911, a howling gale sprang up and three members of the Robinson family were drowned. Two brothers and their cousin set out in their boat alongside the other village fishermen for the mussel grounds at Bardsea, on the Ulverston side of the bay. They worked hard, almost filling the boat with good quality mussels. They turned for home at last, the boat very low in the water, when they ran aground. Before the tide could lift the boat, it was smashed to pieces and the three men drowned. The rest of the fishermen returned safely to Flookburgh as their boats were not so heavily laden.

This tragedy was told to me by a dear old lady who was bred and born in Flookburgh, and for whom I have always had great respect. She said she remembered the night as if it happened yesterday. People were gathered in little groups talking of the disaster, when Mrs. Robinson, wife of one of the drowned men, came out of her cottage in Main Street and said, "What are they all talking about? You all look very sad". Being deaf, she had some difficulty in making out what was being said. "What has happened?" — then she heard her husband's name mentioned and something about a boat being lost. "Oh no! Don't say it's my Ned." All the villagers were silent, until at last one of their number took her gently by the arm and led her towards her cottage and told her what had happened. My friend Ethel said the bodies of the two brothers were found washed up on the sand very early the next morning, but it was a month later before the body of the cousin was picked up by a dredger, whilst dredging the channel at Morecambe. He had left a wife and two small children. In his sermon at the funeral, the vicar remarked that these tragedies often struck more than once as in this case, where two of the victims were brothers and the third their cousin. It was a very sad day for the relatives and for the villagers.

Ethel also told me that nearly all the men in the village were fishermen, and it really was a wonderful sight to see forty or more horses drawing their carts along the mile road, one behind the other, the fishermen calling to one another in their broad dialect. Of course, when they reached the sands, they spread out in different directions, some to fish their fluke nets, others to go cockling but very few went shrimping, as there was no market for them.

Ethel started going to the sands with her dad when she was eight years old, just on Saturdays. Then when she was thirteen years old and left school, she went regularly with him and gained quite a lot of experience on how to set a bawk net to catch flukes, and when the rough seas tore at the nets, her nimble fingers would mend them and make them whole again. Bawk nets are still set by the fishermen in Morecambe Bay, but there are also the bag net and the stream net, though these are rarely used today.

In those days, they were not equipped as we are today. Many women followed the sands and wore clogs, with pieces of oiled cloth wrapped around their legs. They would have an oiled skirt, which their mother had made for them from a piece of calico dipped in oil and dried. An ordinary mackintosh was worn, with a scarf tied around the head. If they were caught in a rain storm or a gale, and rain can be driven at frightening speeds out in the bay, they would be soaked through to the skin, and many a time their clothes would dry on their backs. In summer time, the women wore no shoes or clogs but went barefooted, and even walked down the mile road with their feet bare.

The very early memories of my friend, Ethel, were of setting the nets out on the sands with her dad, Tom, out from Kents Bank on the early morning tide, then later on in the day or in the evening just as dark was coming in, they set out with the horse and cart to fish those nets. As they reached the last few yards of their journey, Ethel jumped off the cart and in her excitement touched the nets and the full length of them lit up. The outline of each mesh was sparkling with brilliant light and all around was lit with a fluorescent glow, the like of which Ethel had never seen before. She was very frightened of this strange light on the nets and in the splashes of water whipped up by the horse's hooves and called to her dad in great alarm. She ran to him and the foxfire, as the fishermen call it, ran with her. "It's nobbut foxfire and it wain't 'ort thi," he said as he approached. Ethel had never heard of it before, but nevertheless, she did see it again occasionally during her time spent out on the sands, fishing along with her father, but it was very rarely.

Such a wonderful sight but it can be very frightening to anyone so young, seeing it for the first time. "Almost like fairyland, when touched," was

Returning home with the shrimp catch. The fish would be boiled, shelled and scalded — and then hawked round the local villages the following day. *(J. Dodgson)*

Shrimping well out in the Bay with the water lapping the horses' bellies. The Flookburgh fisherman on the right was always known as "Sir James". *(J. Dodgson)*

Ethel's description. Foxfire can only be seen when the sea is teeming with fluorescent bodies of tiny organisms — plankton.

Ethel would drive the horse and cart down the channel, while her dad attended to the shrimp net, and in this way, from the age of eight years to thirteen years, she had gained quite a lot of experience.

The following year the first world war was declared; 1914 to 1918. This meant that for a while Ethel and her father had to give up the fishing and do other work, but after the war was over they were back on the sands and Ethel was quite used to going to fish the nets. Wading through the water in the dark to catch the fish with the cramb, a three-pronged handled tool, but the fish had already been trapped by the nets and were lying in shallow water. The first time she stepped into the water, one fluke was startled and shot forward hitting her on the leg so suddenly that she jumped sky-high sending all the other fish swimming back up the shallow dyke away from the net. "Now tha's done it," her dad said, as the startled fish swam about. Time had to be allowed for them to settle down near the front of the net once again. This was a bawk net. Nets, in those days, were knitted in the homes of the fishermen. A big nail was hammered into the wall and then Ethel would be set off knitting with what she called a cowl and a knitting needle, and quite a number of rows had to be done before she was allowed to go out to play with her friends. When the nets were finished, they had to be hung outside, tarred, and allowed to dry before they were used. Nowadays, they are quite different. For instance, they are no longer made of cotton, but of nylon, which more easily entangles the fish and they cannot escape as they may from one of the old nets.

The length of the net is now controlled by law, and must not exceed one hundred and fifty yards, set half-moon shaped with turnpikes at either end to prevent the fish from getting away. The net that Ethel and her dad were using was a bawk net, such as is still carried out in the bay by one or two fishermen during the summer months, but not on the same scale as our forbears, when this type of netting for flukes was so competitive. These nets were set on stakes and the length of net would vary up to the 150 yards allowed. They were set either through a hollow area where the fish would be drawn on the ebb tide, or they would be set out on a bank or bed-end of sand, but here the skill of the fisherman was up against the cunning fluke. Experience told in this profession and the older and wiser fisherman would set this type of net knowing, more or less, that he would have a good catch. First, he would take a thorough look over the area, and decide which way the fluke would leave the sand beds after feeding on the small shellfish, etc., and the way they would make back to deeper water with the ebb of the tide. The long nets had to be moved constantly, because after a few days the fish became wary of the presence of the nets, and catches gradually faded out.

A stiff breeze is helpful whilst netting for flukes, as this cleans the nets from the different kinds of seaweed which are brought in on the tide. In calm weather seaweed can be a real menace to the fishermen, as it clogs the mesh of the nets, making them useless.

Stream nets are set mainly on a dyke foot during the months of March, until early June, and then in August until the end of October, when flukes are plentiful. As the weather gets colder in November and December, the temperature of the sea water drops and the flukes leave the banks where they have been feeding with each tide during the earlier months, and now stay close to the main rivers; the estuaries of the Kent and the Leven. A swift flow of tide is needed for a stream net in which the fluke are meeting the net at speed and are then carried into the bag, and trapped in this way.

The fishermen work independently in Morecambe Bay, and quarrels are not uncommon as each fisherman guards certain pitches with jealousy. All fishermen are rivals — and very few are friends.

The bag is generally set near a dyke on a breast of sand running with a slight slope towards the dyke. The length of the net can vary, usually two or three nets amounting to a length of forty to fifty yards leading down to the bag which when set should be about a foot lower than the net itself. The bag is held in position by two stakes and the net attached to each stake with a piece of string. Inside the bag is an insert, a piece of netting set in such a way as to let the fish in, but which stops them from finding their way out again. This inset the local fishermen call an "inshar" or "inserere". Serere is Latin for "to join", as an insct. It sccms a long way for a Latin word to travel!

The cords of the net are usually tied with strings, not like other kinds of net where the cord is wrapped round the net stakes. Such nets were set on low tides, or just as the tide rose in height. Tails were tied like a shrimp net, at the end, so the fish could be taken out of the bag and the string retied to seal it ready for the next tide.

Once, when Ethel and her father were coming home from the sands, the tide was due. They had worked hard almost to the last minute. She told me her dad was "a divil" for working until the tide was almost at their feet; he made a habit of doing this. For a group of soldiers, it was lucky that Ethel and her father were late starting off for home. The soldiers were walking out on the sands, towards the area where the two had been fishing, one rather late afternoon. Dad spotted the group and said to Ethel, "Lookster theer at that lot, where are thi' guyn", and he set off with the horse and cart to head them off. "Where da-ya think yer guyn?" he said to them. "The tide is comin' and if yer doant be cummin' back, yull-o-be drowned." They turned tail for home as fast as their legs would carry them, and now Ethel and her dad had to get a move on for their own safety, so as to get through the meetings. As soon as they were through, as suddenly as if from nowhere, it was a roaring sea as the two tidal bores met together and covered the sand where just minutes before they had been driving the cart. There would have been no chance at all if they were caught in such an area. When the soldiers reached the shore away from the incoming tide, they thanked Ethel and her

A classic picture that says it all — wet sands, horse-and-cart, a fisherman and his nets, and in the distance the wide expanse of the Bay. Only the oystercatchers are absent. (J. Dodgson)

father and said they deserved a medal! The reply they got was, "I want na medal but I'll gi-ya some advice — Nivver gang out on them sands any mar unless ya nah summet about 'em, or unless yuv gitten a guide, because ya doant nah these sands like we fishermen do. There's quicksands and if ya get in them you'll be a gonner."

Ethel then described her encounter with quicksands to me. "We had a very good horse called Darky, A bit small for the job, and on this particular day we came across some quicksands, and of course, no time could be lost in getting over them. However, we got through without getting stuck, or mired, as the fisherfolk would say. Ethel ran through, but being so young, she was scared stiff, but she knew that to stop in such an area meant you would just go down and down. In bad areas which had to be crossed because there was no alternative route, the fishermen would help the horse, by getting hold of the spokes of the cartwheels and putting all their strength into helping to turn the wheels to enable the horse to struggle through. This Ethel's dad did on this occasion and the game little horse pulled with all his might and came safely out onto the firmer sand. Probably without that extra help, the little horse would not have been able to keep the wheels turning, against the suction of the deadly quicksands. There is always something to be learnt out there on the sands and Ethel added a little more to her knowledge that day.

Fog is really the worst hazard out in the bay. Ethel has seen it so foggy that when sitting on the front of the cart she couldn't see the horse's head, and dad almost always walked in front of the horse, holding the reins. He rode on the cart rarely, when the going was safe. He walked mile after mile across the sands, guiding the horse, then worked for several hours at the nets, or picked up the cockles one by one. Then there would be the long trek back over the sands and the mile walk by road back home, where the fish had to be cleaned. Tom took the fish to the nearby spring to wash them. The icy water firmed the flesh making filleting easier.

When they were going out to the fishing grounds about two in the morning, Ethel, because she was so young, would ride in the feed box and would doze off, lying on the hay. It always amazed her, that even in the dead of night, her father could find the way right to the spot where they had worked the previous day or night. Many a time, he would leave a small wooden peg which he worked down into the sand, not to look so obvious to the other fishermen, but just enough to be seen by him. It would mark a particular good patch of cockles which he would want to work on the next day. He was a very remarkable man. Such experience comes only with living with the sands, day in, day out, and year by year taking notice all the time of the slightest change in anything at all. Failure to take notice of the changes in the direction of the ridges in the sand, made by the tide as it recedes, could mean losing your way, especially after crossing a dyke. Some of the younger fishermen would make a habit of following an experienced old timer, instead of learning for themselves the lore of the sands. In mist or fog, when no landmarks are visible, it is the knowledge gained over the years that stands you in good stead, where otherwise, it could mean tragedy. Sometimes, Ethel told me, her father would give such a youngster a lesson, when he found he was being followed on a misty day. He would lead his horse down a dyke, instead of crossing directly over it, and in this way the youngster would lose the tracks left in the sand from the wheels of the cart. By doing this, Ethel and her dad would have a more peaceful day on the cockle beds.

In winter time, cockling was a cold job, especially in frosty weather. The handles of the jumbo were often frozen and the hands of the person using it would be frozen too. Then batting both arms around the body was the only way to bring the circulaton back, and this in itself was tiring, especially when you had a lot of clothing on, but it is the only way to keep warm out there on the sands. If the hands can be kept warm, then using the jumbo, which is really hard work, will tend to keep the body warm, as long as your hands are kept dry, and this is quite a feat. If you have never had the experience of being out on the sands in winter, you can have no idea how cold it can be. It takes a long time to thaw out when you get near a fire!

Although people of the village were poor at that time, no-one ever went hungry. They were brought up on good wholesome food. Oatmeal porridge with a spoonful of black treacle on top served two purposes — to sweeten and to keep you "regular", and it did both. Often the family would also have "blue milk" with porridge too. This was milk which had the cream skimmed off, for selling separately. Everyone did their own baking and, if you ran short of bread, your neighbour would lend you a loaf until you baked. Then you would give her the loaf back. There was one thing about the villagers, they were all in the same boat. Everyone was poor but if one needed help it was always there, not for pay but for a good turn done back at some future date.

Although there were no good outlets for bulk sales of shrimps, Ethel and her father used to go out now and then, then hurry home and boil the shrimps, shell them, or pick them as we fishermen say, and scald them. Then they would be laid out on a nice clean piece of muslin cloth to cool and dry. The following day Ethel and her mother would set out hawking the shrimps round the local villages from their bogie. The bogie was a shallow wooden box mounted on two great big mangle wheels, which, being made of cast iron, were heavier than the bogie itself. In hot weather a branch would be cut from the hedgerow to waff off the bluebottles as they went along the country roads. There would be one of them batting and the other pushing the heavy bogie.

Sam Taylor, Canon of Carlisle, and at one time vicar of Flookburgh, wrote in *Cartmel, People and Priory* that it needs the pen of a fisherman to do full justice to the moods of the sands, and it is rarely a fisherman's tool. Year in and year out, these men have followed the tides, rising sometimes hours before dawn. Tired they often may be, but strong, healthy and handsome. In times past, they have no doubt had their bad periods, when they lived on what they caught. Let us hope that no catastrophe attacks their means of livelihood to check its steady, hardworking advance in trade and cheerful plain living.

Almost thirty years on, and now the grim forecast of these prominent local fishermen, including myself, is that we are priced out of the markets, and the industry could be dead within ten years, as no youngsters are today following their fathers into the trade, and those same fathers are now well over forty years old. Once they have retired, the industry will die. Cheap imports of cockles from Holland, and shrimps all the way from Japan, have made it very hard for us to compete in marketing our catches. Fishing is a young man's job and if there are no youngsters coming into the trade it cannot survive. It will be sad to see the last of an old tradition, as generations of Flookburgh families, along with fishermen from the surrounding villages, have earned their living from the sea and sands of Morecambe Bay for centuries.

Selling shrimps from a wooden bogie — the branch was for wafting blue-bottles away.

5. Silverdale Fishermen

THE LAST of a dying breed of fishermen to fish with a horse and cart from Silverdale is Eddie Sands. Eddie started fishing in 1928 at the age of twenty-five years, and he remembers that winter as a very severe one indeed, when the whole of the bay was frozen up, even the Kent channel. The tides were very low, but when they started to rise in height, they brought huge chunks of ice towards the shore-line — some of them as high as a house! Another fisherman and a friend of Eddie's was Bill Hartley whose family roots were in Flookburgh. He had come to settle in Silverdale and he and Eddie had set a stream net near to the Kent channel at that time. When they went out to fish it, they found it a solid sheet of ice, and that was in salt water.

In those days they had very good catches well up in the bay and in 1928 the small flukes caught were sold for three pence (old money) per pound. They made a good meal for the larger families there were in those days. The larger flukes were sold at sixpence a pound. That would be two and a half new pence. The nets the fishermen used, Eddie says, had a two and a half inch mesh, whereas today the men who fish the fluke in the bay, myself included, would not think of using anything less than a four and a half to five inch mesh which lets a lot of the smaller fish through to live on and grow.

There were others who made a living from the bay. Mary Holmes, who before her marriage was Mary Dickinson, has lived in one of the shore cottages since she was two years old, and now at the age of 80 years she told me of how she used to go out into the bay with her father, Jackie Dickinson, to set the nets to catch the flukes and gather the cockles. Her father had been a fisherman all his life, as had his parents and grandparents before him.

Webster's were also an old fishing family of Silverdale. They lived in one of the shore cottages, number three. Another fluke fisherman, a tough old bearded, broad-shouldered character, lived in the village and kept his pony on the lots, that's the piece of rocky grassland near the village. The pony stayed out there all year round and seemed to fare quite well, with a few oats and a handful of hay now and then. The lots has now become a council estate, so the fishermen have had to find other fields for their ponies. All his life this old chap had made a living from the bay, either fluke fishing or cockle gathering when the fluke were scarce. He would travel round the villages the next day after catching the fish, hawking it from his pony cart.

The Flookburgh fishermen used to go over the sands to Silverdale, crossing the Kent channel as the early morning tide ebbed and work on until the next tide sent them hurrying to the Silverdale shore, setting their horses off, meaning that they took the horses out of the cart shafts and gave them a feed, and the fisherfolk would have their 'bagging', which would be sandwiches or a pie to keep them going. Then, on the turn of the tide, or as early as they could get out to the cockle beds, they would work for a couple of hours and then make back over the sands to Flookburgh. At one time of day, four or five fishermen would go out with one horse and cart. The outfit would belong to one of the fishermen, and at the end of the week they would have a shareout with the owner having that little bit extra for the keeping of his horse.

Cockles were not always rank, or plentiful, even over at the Silverdale side of the bay, and when they had to be picked up one by one with the cramb, the men were lucky to get a bag each. Cockles were measured in pecks in those early days. In later years, they were measured by the cockle basket with so many quarts to the hundredweight. It was a regular occurrence in those days for the Flookburgh fishermen to cross the Kent channel frequently in spite of the dangers, whenever it was at all possible to ford the river Kent, to work the cockle beds. Some of the fishermen rented cottages in the village rather than be on the move all the time.

My father fished with Eddie Sands for two winters, using Eddie's horse and cart, and dad slept in a caravan down at the old outlook, just outside the village. This was getting late on in the 1930s. After that time, it was getting harder year by year to make a good living from fishing, as deep-sea fishing was knocking the flukeing trade very hard, though trade for cockles was still quite good at the markets. Cockling was much easier if two men worked together; one to rock the wooden jumbo, which brings the cockles to the surface, and the other to pick them up out of the sand with the cramb. The actual permitted size of the jumbo was four foot six inches in length but the fishermen did use much longer boards, up to five or six feet long. They were liable to a fine if they were caught using the longer boards, so if a figure was seen approaching on the sands it could only be the "Watcher" whose job it is to see that the Ministry of Fisheries regulations are carried out. As soon as the "Watcher" was spotted, the men would try to get rid of the long boards. They would gallop off in different directions, as long as they were not caught using the offending boards, otherwise they would have been for the high jump.

Fishermen were always on the look-out for bags, and often this would be quite a problem, as they were needed in such quantities to pack the cockles in for taking to the markets. The hessian bags used by the farmers to buy their provender in were ideal. There were no paper bags and plastic ones were unheard of.

The rag and bone men at that time collected anything and would give children a balloon or some other small toy for a bundle of rags. They often had a stock of hessian sacks and so the fishermen would go to the "raggie" as

Jean Robinson and the author prepare to set out into the Bay in search of cockles. Flookburgh fishermen used to cross the Kent channel to work Silverdale's cockle beds. (Manchester Daily Mail)

they called him and buy for a small sum the sacks to pack the cockles in. I remember dad telling me a tale about when he and Jim Benson, a Flookburgh fisherman, travelled to Lancaster looking for bags. They had heard that there were plenty of raggies there who were always ready to do a deal. They had been told that at Skerton, just outside Lancaster, there was an old chap nicknamed "Bow Wow" — nobody knew why, but he would have all the bags they could possibly want. So off they set in their flat lorry which was a car cut down and which the joiner had made a flat top for, and which was very useful for hawking purposes (most fishermen cum gardeners had had one of these).

On arrival at Skerton, as they were strangers to the area, Jim asked dad to go and try knocking on one of the nearest doors, and ask where "Bow Wow" lived. A young chap answered the door and although he knew the man they were looking for very well, he said to dad, "Tha mon't call 'im by that name, he'll gah mad wi yah". They were not far away from where he lived as they were directed to the end house of a long street near to the river Lune. He was at home and at first sight they could see what a character he was, but Jim Benson was a match for him, and although the man had lots of bags to sell, he wasn't going to let them go without getting his price. After a bit of bantering with Jim, "Bow Wow" said, "Which on yas buying these anyway?" Jim was quick to reply, "Ayther on us or nayther on us, we're not fussy." So a bargain was struck and both customer and dealer were satisfied. Today, the hessian bag is a thing of the past as far as the cockle gatherers are concerned and plastic have taken their place.

Although the bay is so vast and cockle beds can lie over such huge areas, there is a skill in finding the best beds. There were days when the catch was poor and this would unsettle the fishermen, so time was taken, many a time a whole day, all the tide time, scouting round, as they called it. If they found some good patches, it was good to know that they would be having some better catches for a while. That is, if they could keep the area to themselves.

A cockle lies wrong side up in the sand, with a hinge facing upwards. The hinged shellfish work their way into the sand by the "foot" which protrudes from the slightly opened shell, and thus bury themselves. During the summer months, a moss grows out of this and can be seen by the fisherman, particularly when the cockles are plentiful. Now and then the men would try tramping up and down to see if there were many cockles about, as this would bring them to the surface. The best results were secured if the cockle bed could be worked as soon as the tide had ebbed. While the sand is still wet, cockles can be gathered in half the time it takes than if the sand has been allowed to dry out. A very windy day will dry the sand out quickly and make it that much harder to work the jumbo and the cockles don't come to the surface easily.

Fishermen out on the bay were always trying to get the better of each other. None were real pals when they were out there working. If a good patch of mature cockles was found, it was kept a secret from the others. The area would only be visited in the dark, tide permitting, and they would work hard on it before the rest of the fishermen realised what was happening. As soon as the tide ebbed and the higher sandbanks showed, the oystercatchers on the bay made their way down to the cockle beds in large numbers — then the fishermen also had to be on the move.

In 1928 cockle beds were about one and a half miles out from Silverdale shore. The furthest distance one would find cockle beds would be five miles out. With a good horse, a good mover, one could work these beds, as the horse could do about five miles an hour and that would give time to make a good catch before tide time.

Although fishing went on all through the week, orders were mostly sent off at the weekend. A few orders might be sent on Monday or Tuesday, but most bags would be kept on the shore above the tide line and covered with a few empty bags. They took no harm for a few days and when the tide came in close to the shore, the fishermen would carry a few bucketfuls of sea water to throw over the cockles to help keep them fresh, and to keep them from drying out.

With the plentiful supply of the cockles gathered by the Flookburgh men, the railway company found it worth while to lay on a few wagons for the despatch of the cockles. When the wagons were fully loaded, a passenger train destined for the market towns of Bradford, Manchester, Leeds or Liverpool would back into the siding and hook up, and away they would go. Most of these cockles went away on commission, as there were no regular arrangements as to sales orders or payment. It was a gamble whether you got owt or nowt, and frequently the fishermen would receive a "condemned note" saying the cockles were not just up to standard. But on average, the wholesalers were pretty fair.

When cockling in the bay became less profitable, Eddie set fluke nets and hawked the flukes around the surrounding districts from his van. Flukes which feed on the young cockles called "whe-at" have a much nicer flavour than those caught a long way up the bay away from the cockle beds. He set the bawk nets during the summer as the flukes go out more onto the banks where young cockles feed, mostly at night time, and catches are always better following the night tide. Everything which lives on the tide will follow the tide, whether it be night or day. They feed almost to the last minute as the tide doesn't cover the higher banks for long.

Apart from the 1939-45 war, when fishing was not possible from the east coast ports, fluke fishing was a dying trade. But when the war started, there was a shortage of fish from the deep-sea fishing, and the fluke was then graded as a flat-fish along with plaice which was dear to buy. This really made the Flookburgh and the other bay fishermen, because they could now sell their catches anywhere at good prices.

Eddie Sands did most of his fishing from Red Brick Farm on the outskirts of Silverdale, but as time went on Eddie found himself the last surviving fisherman, working the sands alone, and as I well know there is no pleasure being out there on your own, especially on the very dark, moonless nights, so in 1953 Eddie decided to call it a day.

The life of the fisherfolk is a hard one but to those who have responded to the call of the sands and the sea, it is a good healthy life. Living close to nature, as we do, our minds are free from the strain of this modern society, and our interest in simple things, our humour and generosity, show through to the general public who, these days, find it hard to believe that our breed of men do still exist.

An ancient ceremony was revived at Silverdale of "beating the bounds". The ceremony had not been performed since 1895. This took place in 1977 on the 24 September and 8 October. It was revived by the parish council to crown the Silver Jubilee Celebrations, but because the original boundary was several miles in length, over some difficult ground, and included a stretch of Morecambe Bay, it was decided to spread the event over two days.

The most difficult part of the journey was tackled on the Saturday and this included a journey along the Kent Channel, in an inflatable rubber dinghy. Many supporters followed us for most of the way, and they got quite a wetting. I was asked to go along to make sure the party kept out of the dangerous areas.

The organisers tried to follow the exact route and ceremony recorded in the history books, with the symbolic blessing of the triangular pile of boundary stones of which Silverdale has four. The seaward boundary of the Parish of Silverdale extends from the County wall beyond the Cove, in a straight line across the bay towards Guides Farm at Grange over Sands, until it reaches the Kent channel, then south along mid-channel until is is intersected by a line drawn from Pidgeon Cote Lane on the Humphrey Head side of the bay, and then eastwards towards Bardswell. There is one unusual feature of the 'bounds', that the western boundary runs down the centre of the Kent channel, and as the channel moves, sometimes from one side of the bay to the other, so the Silverdale bounds move too.

Enjoyable as the walk was, there were moments in the Kent channel when the flow was so swift, running in "gilimers" (that is a dialect word used by the fishermen and means that the channel is runing like rapids in a river), we thought that at any moment the dinghy would overturn, but we made it "on the line" according to plan. Those who followed us watched from the edge of the channel, and remarked that it made them dizzy to watch us battling our way through the rough waters. The party became fearful on the homeward journey too, when, on the turn of the tide, we were crossing gulleys, knee deep in water, with the sand moving slightly beneath our feet, and they were all thankful when we reached the safety of the shore once again and our feet were once more on the solid earth.

Like most villages around the coast of Morecambe Bay, Silverdale has been connected with fishing for centuries and at one time had its own small shrimping fleet. No doubt, when that side of the bay silted up considerably, the fishermen were no longer able to use their boats, and started fishing with the horse and cart, for cockles, plaice and fluke and other fish.

Jenny Brown's Point is not named after one of the local maidens, but after an old steam engine used many years ago in the local quarry when an unsuccessful attempt was made to reclaim part of the bay by building a breakwater. A section of this wall still remains today and has been brought to light during the last few years by the movement of the river Kent. On old maps, the point is called Silverdale Point.

When the tide is in, unwary bathers may suddenly fall into deep water as the tide weakens the banks of the river and the banks cave in, at times with the roar of a cannon. It is said that when one bank collapsed, fishermen from Silverdale saw revealed the mummified body of a man still clasping a riding whip, the salt in the sand having preserved his body from decay.

6. Morecambe

A LITTLE further along the coast at Morecambe the original fishermen were called crofters, farmers combining their work with fishing, according to Sam Baxter, similar to their rivals here across the bay at Flookburgh. Although Sam is not what you would call an old fisherman, he is probably one of the oldest surviving but still comparatively young.

Sam's memories of what he has been told of the early days are pretty accurate and he stands by them. Settlers came down to the area from Scotland and there were already a few original families and there are still a few of them left today. They are the Baxters, Sam's own family, the Woodhouses and the Willacys, who were originally fisherman farmers, with the fishing done with the horse and cart. They set stake nets for flukes and did a lot of push netting or hand netting for shrimps. Gathering mussels was a busy occupation, and these were all transported by horse and cart. The mussel scars or skeers were close to the shore and some of the fishermen used a bicycle and carried the catch home on the cross-bar which was far easier than carrying them on his back.

In those days the fisherfolk had to pay a levy to the monasteries as they owned all the fishing rights on the Morecambe side of the bay. Later on, at the dissolution of the monasteries, the fishing rights went to the Lords of the Manor of Heysham, and the levy had to be paid to them for the privilege of fishing in the bay.

Eventually, the men started using rowing boats and punts to do a bit of fishing, but this never really took off in a big way. There was only limited local trade to deal with the catches. Often, the fish had to be carried to Lancaster and hawked round the streets. Business was in a very small way until the railways came. This opened up the new markets inland for the fishermen, and they decided to drop the farming side of their work and have bigger boats built so that they could supply the new markets. The boats were thirty to thirty-six feet, and were crewed by father and son or two brothers, and so were family affairs. This new venture brought trade to the small boat-building yard at Arnside on the northern coast of the bay.

The larger craft enabled the men to fish much farther afield and they fished the upper parts of the bay for shrimps and went down the bay towards the Irish Sea for sprawns, which are pink shrimps the same size as the Morecambe Bay brown shrimp but thought by some people tastier. One of the hazards of trawling for the pink shrimp was that it feeds on stony, gravelly areas, and nets were often caught up on the boulders but they were usually freed fairly quickly by reversing the trawler and pulling the net free. They were very lucky if they got away with half an hour's trawling before finding the net fast among these boulders. In fact, the lower they went down the coast, the more frequently they found themselves faced with the boulders.

As a lad, Sam recalls that fishing for the sprawns was more profitable than fishing for brown shrimps. They were sent off to the markets of the Lancashire and Yorkshire towns in big barrels being mixed with salt to preserve them. Even so, there were still plenty of brown shrimps being caught and picked in Morecambe, in the upper reaches of the bay where they feed on the sandy bottom, but the sales of these were not to be compared with the sales of the sprawns. The fishermen could not make a living from the shrimps alone. The men felt they were getting a raw deal from the wholesale markets and so the Morecambe Trawler Society was formed.

All the fishermen of the village would go out in the early hours of the morning and several hours later would come home with their catch, unload, and then go to bed, while their wives and daughters — and there were often quite a number of daughters, as it was not uncommon at that time for there to be as many as twelve or thirteen children in a family — would spend their time picking and packing the shrimps ready for when father got up about tea time to take the shrimps to the station where they were put on the train for the inland markets. There was often little return for all their work and sometimes there was just a note saying that the shrimps were not fit for human consumption which was a minor tragedy for the family. As these "Condemned" notes came with increasing frequency, everyone was getting more and more disheartened and began to think they were conned, twisted out of their payment, and no doubt they were in most cases, so a few of the fishermen got together and with what bit of money they had at the time bought an old derelict woodyard bounded by four cobbled walls. A building was put up which has since been added to. They then started doing their own marketing in 1919 but trading really started in 1920 when they employed a manager who was also a fisherman.

Herbert Willacy who was the first secretary-manager was a fisherman, and became full time manager. They formed their own Board of Directors, all of them fishermen. One of them, Walter Baxter, was also a councillor and later became Mayor of Morecambe. Herbert Willacy also became Mayor at a later date. This was the start of things which got them off the ground. Doing their own marketing gave them a much better deal, but what really put them on their feet was the introduction of the potted shrimp. Remembering that these were the days before refrigeration, and as we all know that shell fish without refrigeration would not keep very long, they found that by putting the picked shrimps in butter and spices they would keep longer. In conjunction with Young's Seafoods of London, who were the first people to start selling potted shrimps, the Morecambe Bay trawler-men who first

Morecambe fishermen in search of their catch. Today the town has only some fifteen full-time fishermen compared with over a hundred in the 1920s.

started potting them built up a regular trade. This meant that the trawlermen of Morecambe now had a steady job, although no one made a fortune out of it, but it was something coming in regularly. This was around the mid 1920s right up to the war years.

At that time there were more than one hundred fishermen in Morecambe but by the mid 1930s when Sam Baxter started fishing the number had dropped to about forty. Today there are around fifteen full time, and Sam is often asked why there are so few fishermen following the sands. The reason is that in the early days there were big families with several lads and very little in the way of other work, so it was either follow the fishing or nothing. There was no dole money so they had to go fishing irrespective of whether they caught owt or nowt, because that was the only thing to do. As soon as the lads left school, they would start fishing with their father or brother as there was no other option. Nowadays all that has changed and those who follow the sands do so because they prefer it, as Sam has done all his life. There are only one or two children in the families of these days so fishermen are few and far between.

Sam recalls that when he started fishing there were some trawlers modified with small petrol engines. Most were still under sail though there were some that had both, so if there was a stiff breeze the engine could be cut out, probably to save fuel. Although Sam agrees that fishing in those days was a hard life, the changes over the years have not made it much easier. It is still a hard life. In the days before the engine, there are stories told of how the fishermen had to row all the way to the fishing grounds and back again, if there was no wind, even all the way back from near Blackpool! The tide could be a little help, but it was a four or five hour job. It was certainly hard graft and they would be working their gear in twenty or thirty fathoms, and the gear all had to be manhandled, as there were no capstans or such to ease the job.

The catches of shrimps have always been boiled on board the trawlers in sea-water, and the fishermen of Morecambe believe that this method gives them that little bit of extra flavour, over our shrimps at Flookburgh, although the shrimps may be caught at the same grounds. Our catches are brought home alive to be boiled in fresh water. The Morecambe men may have the edge on our shrimps for flavour but it is a fact that over the years ours have always been easier to pick as the Flookburgh women will agree.

A big drawback for the Morecambe fishermen is that they have no jetty. There is no harbour and the boats have to be left on an open beach, and in rough weather they have to be visited on each tide to make sure that nothing has gone amiss and to bale out and see to the moorings. There is always the danger of a boat breaking away and being smashed against the sea wall. Almost all the fishermen have had this happen to them in their lifetime. Sam has lost two boats in this way. Because of this, boat owners have very heavy insurance premiums to pay, but to offset this there is the advantage of being able to sail in and out at practically any state of the tide. If there are plenty of shrimps to be caught in the upper reaches of the bay, you can sail out on the last of the ebb, when the tide is going out, and get a few hours fishing with the shelter of the sandbanks and get back before the sandbanks are covered with the tide, and it starts to get rough. The only trouble is that the catches have to be carried from the boats across the beach. With very big catches though, a tractor is at hand to transport the fish from the boats to the shore. Shrimp picking is done on the premises of the Morecambe Trawlers Society, and the pickers are mostly pensioners. There is room to seat about thirty people for this rather specific job of shrimp picking, but Sam tells me that at the present time there are only about fifteen regular pickers and they are all women. They are not employed by the society, but are paid for the amount they pick, and are free to come and go as they please which suits the pickers very well.

A great variety of fish is caught out in Morecambe bay, and is sold fresh and frozen from the premises. Flukes, plaice, shrimps, whitebait, codling, sprats and dabs all find their way onto the slabs in the wholesale store. When the society was formed in 1920 a shop was also built next door for selling retail to the public, but this never paid its way. As the saying goes, "There's now't so queer as folk". People preferred to come into the warehouse. When told they would have to go into the shop, they replied, "Oh, we are not going there, fish isn't as fresh as it is here." In actual fact, all the fish was from the same catch, but there was no convincing them, and most of the customers still came to the warehouse. Eventually, as the shop next door was not a success, the members thought they could well do without it. At that time anyway most of their trade was wholesale. It was leased off and the same people still have it to this day. This was in 1971.

Sam has been fishing all his life, and he told me of an accident he had whilst out fishing with his brother. They had had a very hard winter, and had caught nothing for weeks. As the time went by and it was getting into May, with poor catches, they decided to try their luck in the first channel close to Morecambe and Silverdale. Some good catches were netted. They decided to "strike while the iron was hot" as the old saying goes, as the catches were mainly plaice always in good demand, so, instead of going to bed, when he reached home, he just grabbed a little something to eat and went eagerly out on the next tide, very early in the morning. Once again there was quite a good catch but by this time it was almost 7 am, and Sam was very tired. He was barely able to keep his eyes open, and when hauling the net into the boat at low-water, his attention wandered and the trawl rope round the mechanised capstan became fouled up with a riding turn in it. He was always taught as a lad that should this ever happen he must stop the capstan as a first step for safety. Of course, as Sam was over-tired he was careless and instead of stopping the capstan he tried to kick the rope clear with his foot. The rope whipped round his foot and the next moment his foot and leg were trapped by several turns of the rope, and Sam was thrown on his back against the side of the boat. Fortunately his brother who was down below had the sense to stop the engine, but the damage had been done. Luckily there was another boat fishing close by which came to their aid, and the men cut Sam loose. As a result of this accident, Sam spent three weeks in Lancaster Infirmary and was then told that nothing further could be done. He would be a cripple for life. In fact he was a cripple, always in great pain and hardly able to walk. His knee was the main problem, but Sam was not the sort of person to give up easily. One of his friends who was in a position of authority in the St John's Ambulance Brigade, in London, arranged for Sam to have a consulation in London and then he went to the Seamen's Hospital in Greenwich where he had an operation. Although his leg is still unstable, the continual pain he had suffered soon disappeared and he was able to walk again, drive a vehicle and do most things anyone else can do. The only thing is he cannot kneel down. He can live a practically normal life. The one thing he could not do was to go back to sea. With a stiff knee, he would be a liability on a trawler, but to be out of work at fifty years old with a wife and four children and knowing no other trade than fishing things looked very black.

He was still chairman of the Morecambe Trawlers Society though, so

One of Morecambe Bay's famous sunsets — at the close of a stormy day. The photograph was taken from a point close to Morecambe's Central Pier. _(T. Parker)_

while convalescent he would go down to the Trawlers Society to pass the time on. When he was in the warehouse, as I mentioned earlier, people would come in and would ask if they could buy fish and shrimps, so after thinking it over Sam put up a table and put out a box or two of fish and placed his cap there to put the takings in, and opened the door to the public. It took off in a big way from that day on. It now takes five of them to keep the sales going from the warehouse. On the retail side, Sam found he had created a job for himself, and he was approached with the view of his becoming manager as well and he has been doing this ever since. He likes the work, and can do very much as he likes but with all his experience at sea and on land, he says, with a glint in his eye, "It's easier to catch the fish than to sell them".

Nowadays, half of the fleet trawls for shrimps all the time, while the other half, fish trawl and go much farther afield than Morecambe Bay, where they can catch plaice, dover sole, codling, skate and whiting, all of which can be caught in the same trawl net and sorted and gutted on the boats before they get back to the shore. The autumn of 1980 was the best season for codling that Sam can remember. He also tells of the time when the Morecambe trawler men found times so hard that they had to move to other waters to try to make a living. They would sail up to the Solway Firth to fish for herring. They lived on the boats as Sam, then aged 16 years, well remembers, sailing up to Maryport and Solway after the herring aboard a 35 ft. prawner and living very rough. There was a little stove in the fore-castle, and there was only enough room for father, uncle and Sam to crouch down. They couldn't even sit upright, much less stand up, but they slept, and did their work in that confined space. To Sam, it seemed like working down a coal mine. Meals had to be as simple as possible, bacon and egg, and plenty of herring of course.

Sam would rather forget the next tale of his experience as ship's cook. The first meal of the day was egg and bacon, and he would cut the bread nice and thick, fry it crispy, serving the egg and bacon on top of the bread, saying to his father, "There's yer plate", thinking of saving the washing up. After a while, he asked, "Do ya want some more bacon?" His dad said "Yes". "Well, pass us yer plate then." "Nay lad, I've eaten it," said dad.

When they reached the herring grounds, and the first catch came aboard, Sam would sort out a few nice plump herrings and would fry them for the next meal. Then, as they reached the harbour after their successful trawl, they would have a fry-up of eggs and bacon. Father took a taste of the bacon and said, "Ay lad tha's fried it in't herring fat." These are the things which can be remembered and laughed about years afterwards.

About fifty years ago, Morecambe fishermen used to fish for flukes well up the bay as far as Arnside, trawling up on the flood tide, timing it so that they reached the viaduct just as the tide had lost its force. To get the timing wrong could land you in serious trouble, as one young fellow found out to his cost. Putting his gear out too soon, he reached the viaduct just floating up on the tide. There was no wind to fill his sail, and the anchor wouldn't hold as the force of the tide was too great. His trawler finished up crossways to the viaduct and filling with water, and sinking. He saved himself by climbing up the mast onto the railway viaduct and walked ashore. It was lucky that he could climb the mast, or he would have been drowned.

The last time Morecambe trawler men had to leave their own fishing grounds for other regions was fifteen years ago when some of them went down to Mostin in North Wales and fished there for a couple of months in the winter-time.

Old Captain Alan, who was a well-known Morecambe fisherman and quite a character, used to take his sailing boat with his wife and family and his furniture, pots and pans — in fact everything useful — for a long stay up at a cottage he had in Maryport. There he would fish, until things improved down in Morecambe Bay, when he would move back to his home again.

In those days there was no dole money and the fishermen had to do whatever they could to make some kind of a living. Today, if their catches are poor, they are fortunate enough to be able to draw the dole, but the Flookburgh fishermen, because of their unique way of fishing without boats but with tractors, are not able to get this help, when there is neither fish nor cockles to be gathered. A new insurance act came in during 1948 and until then the Morecambe men were in the same boat as the Flookburgh lads. The Act seems unfair to the Flookburgh lads, to say the least. They even formed their own fishermen's society, but could get no satisfaction. Sam has divided views on the men being able to draw the dole money, because when catches drop below a certain level the men lay off fishing for a while, and this means no fish coming into the Society at regular intervals to keep it going.

Morecambe had a marvellous fishermen's choir, which goes back to the early days of the century. Many of the fishermen are Methodist by religion and attended Clarence Street Chapel known as the fishermen's chapel. The minister thought it a good idea for the fishermen to form a choir and it soon became very popular around the area. In fact, when the terrible tragedy befell the families in Flookburgh, the choir gave a concert to raise money towards a fund for the relatives of the drowned men.

During the first world war the choir gradually died away, but it was reformed when hostilities were over and they actually broadcast on BBC radio. They didn't just sing, they took over the whole church service. There were two or three of them who could preach a good sermon, and at least half a dozen good soloist singers. Sam was lucky enough to be a member of the choir, because it continued right up to the second world war. Sadly, in 1940 members of the choir were called up for H.M. Services, and after the war was over there were not enough fishermen left to form another choir. Their last performance was just as popular as their first one had been. Sam as the youngest member of the choir can tell of the times they used to travel all over the north of England, giving concerts, taking services . . . they were very, very popular. Quite an experience for someone of Sam's tender age.

In a fishing community everyone dreads the news of a tragedy, but Morecambe has been fortunate in these latter years. Tragedy did hit Sam's family though, when his father's younger brother who had just left school started fishing with his dad. The lad, named Sam, had just had his fourteenth birthday and had been given a pocket watch of which he was very proud. It was his first day out fishing, and they were off to Piel near Barrow-in-Furness trawling for plaice. Young Sam was standing on the deck of their sailing boat. It was long before the days of engine power. Father wanted the young lad to have a chance of showing off his watch, so he said to his son, "What time is it Sam?" and the lad proudly pulled his watch out of his pocket and told his dad the time. "Well mi' lad it's time we were making for home then." As he pushed the tiller over and steered the boat round, young Sam was caught unawares and as the boat was leaning over, he lost his balance and fell overboard. His father managed to grab his son by the jersey, as he was floating past. The boat was under sail and still going at speed and in order to drop the sails he would have to let go of his son. He held on to the lad as long as he could muster the strength, but eventually in order to drop the sail he had to let go of the lad and never saw anything of him again.

Another tragedy was that of Walter Baxter in the early 1930s. He was fishing out in the bay in his boat named *The Shrimp Girl,* a brand new boat. No one knows exactly what happened to Walter as the other fishermen found the boat empty, with the net half in the water and half out, so they just presumed that he had been standing on the deck hauling in his net and had slipped and fallen overboard. His body was eventually picked up.

Just after the war, in the 1940s, a young fellow called John Byron had only just started fishing. He used to take parties of anglers out into the bay at weekends. He was not of a fishing family but was very keen on the sea and had a good boat. He had a full boat load of anglers and was anchored out in the bay, when he slipped on the deck and fell overboard. None of the anglers knew anything at all about boats. They didn't even know how to pull the anchor in or even how to start the engine. This happened just out from Heysham and luckily they were seen from the shore and were rescued.

Very few people have lived to tell their own tale of when they fell overboard, but in 1970 a Morecambe fisherman whose right arm was paralysed, and who cannot swim, fell overboard while fishing in the bay very early one Saturday morning. He managed to grab the side of the boat with his left hand, wriggling out of his thigh boots as they filled with water. They had become so heavy with the water that they were threatening to drag him down to the depths. Slowly and determinedly, he worked his way round to the stern of the boat where he was able with an all-out effort to throw his left leg over the stern, while with his left hand he managed to pull himself aboard after several attempts. He then lay in the bottom of the boat, recovering his breath and saying his prayers. Ernie Nicholson had been fishing for plaice and was about to return with his catch when the accident occurred. He said he was leaning over to fix the winch, when he lost his balance and fell overboard. He reckoned he was in about thirty feet of water at the time, and it was fairly cold but luckily the sea was calm. After returning home wet through to the skin and telling his parents of his ordeal he had breakfast and went to bed. Ernie is a keen fisherman and also a net maker, who served his time with the Morecambe Trawlers Society, under Mr. John Baxter. He now has a shop in Lancaster Road, Morecambe.

The last tragedy in Morecambe Bay happened four years ago. A young chap named David Green, who was a member of the Morecambe Trawlers Society and fast becoming one of the best fishermen in the Society, was so keen and a real trier that even when the rest of the men gave up as the whitebait were not coming up into the bay, he kept going. He was always very optimistic thinking that the fish would be there if he tried for long enough. He obviously liked his job and was dedicated to going out week after week all through the winter. Then when it got around to April, he came into the shop with a good catch and said to Sam, "I've cracked it Mr. Baxter, we're alright now".

He went out the next day and had a young lad with him on the boat. He was doing what is called bogey netting for whitebait. The boat lies at anchor with the net slung underneath it in a very hard tide. The method of fishing these bogey nets was to have a dinghy fastened astern with a rope to the boat. The fisherman would get into the dinghy, and slack the rope back towards the tailend until he and the dinghy were level with it. All this time, as the shoal of whitebait passed under the boat and great quantities of the fish found themselves swimming into the mouth of the net, the tailend of the net became very heavy.

David watched and knew he had a good catch. The tide was still running very strong and as he tried to lift the heavy catch into the dinghy it slewed round and got across the tide and filled with water and was swept away. The lad in the trawler was quite inexperienced and didn't know what to do in these terrible circumstances. What he should have done was to have chopped everything away, so as to make the boat free. However, he did have the presence of mind, as there was a radio in the boat, to call the Formby Lifeboat at Liverpool who in turn called Sam at Morecambe. He was the Lifeboat Secretary at the time, and the inshore lifeboat was turned out straight away but of course it was too late. David was drowned and was picked up later that evening on a sand-bank, just opposite the Central Pier. This was all so terribly sad as he was so well-known and such a nice lad too. He was just thirty years old. All such tragedies are sad occasions, but this one seemed worse as he was so well liked by everyone.

One of the worst tragedies associated with Morecambe Bay happened on Monday, 3 September 1894, when the sailing yacht *Matchless* sailed out into the bay on a calm day and never returned. Twenty-five lives were lost, and the cause of the tragedy was never known. It was believed that a strong breeze came up, as it can so suddenly in a bay such as this, and the yacht blew over. The victims were holiday makers from Lancashire and Yorkshire towns. A few days later the Fisherman's Association published a letter of condolence signed by seven of its members, Walter Baxter, John Birkett, James Allen, John Gardner, Luke Woodhouse, Joseph Bell and their Secretary Edward Gardner. It was sent to relatives of the people who were lost in the accident and told of the fishermen's inexpressible grief. The tragedy was one of those unaccountable happenings beyond the control of human beings. All the crew of the yacht were fully experienced and this added to the unaccountability of the loss of the yacht with all aboard her.

In the days of sail, regular trips from Morecambe and Grange over Sands were organised across and around the bay, In those days there were at least seven or eight landing stages in Morecambe, compared with the two they have today. Grange had two wooden piers from which boats could operate at high and low water. Smaller rowing boats would be hired out on the river Kent which ran close in to the shore. At low tides it was possible to sail down the river and meet the tide and sail back with it provided they were supervised by a knowledgeable person. These pleasure trips were possible during the summer months, when weather and tide permitted, ideally on the morning's ebb tide across to Morecambe and back on the evening incoming tide.

The Burrow family followed the bay for their livelihood, and had a fine yacht named *Eileen Alana,* also a large motor launch capable of carrying twenty to thirty persons. The fare for the trip across the bay was one shilling and sixpence each way, or three shillings return, with a long stay in Morecambe, but the people coming from the Morecambe side to Grange could only stay in Grange for an hour or so at the most and then sail back on the ebb tide.

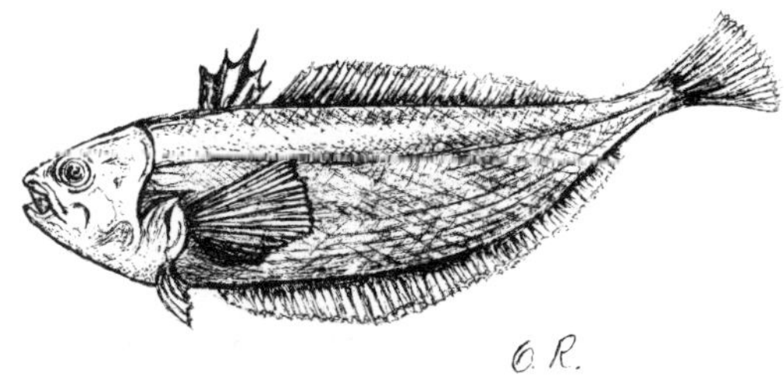

It was a wonderful leisurely life for those people who owned their own yachts or other craft, as there was always the chance of a sail in the estuary or on the river Kent. The only drawback was that there was no lifeboat. Morecambe relied on the RNLI or the lifeboat of either Fleetwood or Blackpool, but after the terrible loss of life on that tragic day in 1894, some of the local people of Morecambe raised enough money to purchase a lifeboat of their own and handed it over to the Morecambe fishermen for safekeeping. The fishermen manned the lifeboat and later formed the Morecambe Fishermen's Lifeboat Association in the 1890s and it is still in being today, so Morecambe is one of the very few places if not the only one which has its own "private" lifeboat. Since 1967 the fishermen have also had the RNLI inshore rescue lifeboat too, but for almost one hundred years they depended on their own boat. During the last one hundred years they had had to replace their lifeboat and in that time they have had three. The present one is called *The Sir William Priestly,* and was given by the late Lady Priestly of Bradford, in memory of her husband. She presented it to Morecambe in 1930 and it is still in their possession.

To get back to Sam, he had not only been connected with fishing all his life, but also with the administrative side of it too. He represented the local fishermen on the Lancashire and Western Sea Fisheries Committee, the Fisheries Organisation Society and various other bodies, and has been the chairman of the Sea Fisheries Committee for ten years. He also has a patrol vessel named after him. It is based in Fleetwood. Seven years ago a letter arrived for Sam from the Prime Minsister, who at that time was James Callaghan, saying that Sam had been awarded the MBE for services rendered to the fishing industry, and that really 'made his day'. It was a very nice thing to have happened and Sam travelled down to London and Buckingham Palace where the Queen Mother presented the awards. Sam was strongly affected by all this and when he was introduced to the Queen Mother and she asked him where he lived, he replied "Morecambe Maam". She could have asked many things said Sam but she said, "And are there plenty of shrimps about at Morecambe?" Sam thought that was wonderful.

That was in February seven years ago, and that made all of Sam's life, both at sea and on the managerial side of things, all the hard dedicated work, and long hours attending meetings, really worth-while.

Morecambe was previously known as Poulton-le-Sands, and in 1841 the census showed the population to be seven hundred — of these, many were fishermen. It was not until 1848 with the opening of the railway that the old village of Poulton became known as Morecambe, which name is of Celtic origin and signifies "a bay". The Morecambe Bay Harbour and Railway Company was formed at this time and work began on improving the town. The sea wall was built in 1849 and became the beginning of the promenade. The North Western Railway company was responsible for the venture, and now thousands of visitors joined in the rush for the coast as the sea bathing fever caught on. During the summer months Morecambe and Heysham prepared to receive the throngs of holiday-makers and would set out their stalls, but by the end of the summer would return to a normal life.

Morecambe also has the honour of being a pioneer in public illumination schemes, as after the first world war these were started as peace celebrations. Candle-lit containers were hung from trees and buildings along the promenade, and were lit each night by groups of local youths who received one penny a dozen for their labour. Today Morecambe illuminations are a bonus for the holiday-makers. The whole of the promenade and Happy Mount Park come alive when some well-known personality throws the famous switch to herald the start of a brilliant illuminations season.

Poulton Square and the surrounding area is the oldest part of Morecambe, and some of the original buildings still stand. Some romantic tales are told of the old Smuggler's Den pub, and some of them have no doubt a grain of truth in them, although recorded history does not connect the pub with all the fearful happenings of bygone days. There is plenty of evidence though that smuggling did take place on Poulton Sands, and rumours connected Poulton Hall, on the site of which Morecambe Market now stands, with these illegal activities. There is a fascinating theory that a bricked up archway in the cellar of the Smuggler's Den may have been the entrance to a tunnel leading to the Hall. Guesswork, of course, but certainly it has romantic possibilities.

In the public bar of the Smuggler's Den, the lounge and the den are full of unusual reminders of those times. From one vantage point the actual bar counter gives a strong illusion of a ship's bows. Attractive stained glass windows show smuggling scenes of the seventeenth and eighteenth centuries. A splendid model of a local trawler *The Margaret* adorns the mantlepiece in the lounge. A ship's wheel and numerous pieces of brassware, mostly marine, form part of the scheme of decoration, and illumination is provided by authentic ships' lanterns. As I sat over a glass of ale, chatting to some of the local fishermen who regularly come to the pub, I could feel the atmosphere all around me, and I could well imagine what it must have been like in the past. Legend has it that a ghost walks the Smuggler's Den. Smugglers are reputed to have carried their booty into the pub, through an underground passage in the cellar, as long ago as the fifteenth century. The ghost is said to be one of the old smugglers, named Sam, who was buried alive in the tunnel and left to die after a quarrel over the division of the booty. His mates fled to escape the law. Sam is still looking for those who deserted him so the story goes.

A local and regular customer at the pub, convinced he had seen the ghost as he sat in the corner of the bar, says he caught sight of it out of the corner of his eye. He was so frightened by the apparition that his friends had to take him home. It didn't stop at that though. The son of the landlord was drinking with the fellow one evening and accused him of being frightened of the dark. The man hotly denied this, and bet that he dare spend the night in the pub's haunted cellars. Five pounds was the wager and it was accepted on the understanding that the money should go to charity. When the other regulars heard of the bet, many of them put their stake in.

To see that everything was ship-shape and Bristol fashion, as the saying goes, the landlord insisted that an indemnity card should be signed, accepting all responsibility with no liability on the management. In theory, anything could have happened. The conditions of the bet were that he had to be sober and all he was allowed to take down with him was a box of matches and a hand bell to ring if his nerves cracked. As the time of his vigil approached he became more and more nervous, and wished he had not been so foolish as to start the wager. But at the appointed hour, down he went into the dark and fearsome cellar. He didn't relish the idea of meeting up with Sam in the pitch dark, in the middle of the night, in the centuries old tunnels beneath the pub.

The ghost of smuggler Sam in the cellar of the Smuggler's Den public bar.

He emerged from his solitary confinement nine hours later. His eyes, alternately staring and blinking in the daylight, looked out from his pinched and blood-drained face. Fright showed in every part of his being, and not a word could be dragged out of him. A tankard of ale was offered to him, which he took at last with shaking hands. The landlord decided that the only thing to do was to take him home and give him a tot of brandy and let him sleep off the effects of his ordeal. The landlord said he wouldn't have spent an hour down there for a hundred pounds, let alone nine! Many of the patrons of the pub have said they have seen Sam wandering around, still looking for those fellow smugglers who deserted him, no doubt. One good thing to come out of this affair was that the charity benefited by the goodly sum of fifty pounds.

Some weeks later a little light was thrown onto how he spent the time in the cellar. It seems he thought that to use the matches to best advantage he would strike one at intervals, and to this end he would have to count them. He had just begun to tip the matches into his hand, when he was startled by a peculiar tapping, knocking and moaning. His thoughts of course were of Sam, and the matches were scattered in all directions. In his normal state, he would have realised that the sounds could have been transmitted through the ground into the cellar and easily explained. No, he was in anything but a normal state, and used several of the precious matches, leaving him with more time in the dark, later. One thing he is sure about is that he will not be spending any more nights in the cellar of the Smuggler's Den.

A cockle and henpennies (Macoma Balthica).

7. When the Wind Blows

A STRONG WIND along with a high tide can play havoc with dwellings near the sea, hurling great waves laden with shingle and stones upon them, smashing the embankments and breakwaters, and sending the sea to flood the low-lying parts of the land. Floods in many places on the coast will be remembered by all, but Morecambe has had more than its fair share in the past years. Records show that on 18 October in the year 1720, the flood was described as the greatest sea flood that had ever occurred in the memory of living man. The high tide, backed by a fierce gale-force wind, came in at midday and flooded many houses. Boats had to be used to rescue the people from their homes. It drove ships of ninety tons from their moorings and swept them into King's Meadow. The flood water found its way into the warehouses and the Custom House, where the tobacco was all damaged but the wine and brandy, being in bottles, was saved. It entered many buildings and beat down walls, and did great damage about the town. The wind fell that night, and the next night the tide was not so high and everyone thought the worst was over, but the following day the storm rose again and the tide ran as high as the day before causing great damage to fences and property and overflowing the land all along the coast. It found its way into the barns, spoiling the hay and corn, and drowned the sheep and cattle. It was like an inland sea in Thernham and other low lands where it remained for several days until it gradually drained away. Eight persons were drowned on Thernham Moss, and many people were without food or drink for forty-eight hours. The ships at Sunderland Point rode out the storm, but several were lost about Piel Island. Had this happened in the night and not the daytime, many more people would have been drowned in their beds, and the loss would have been much greater. Many people lost everything and went inland to beg.

To the farming folk of the lonely saltings and the birch-grown peat bogs of the Foulshaw farms, at the furthermost tip of the Kent Estuary, the great flood disaster of 1907 was caused by a racing tide, backed by a midnight gale, which breached the dykes and swept over the mosslands. Dawn saw devastation. There was water as far as the eye could see. The grim light filtered through six great gaps in the bank which had given in all directions. The whole Lyth Valley showed up like one vast lagoon. All herdsmen were at work saving what they could of the stock. A sheep crawled on a fence within inches of the swirling water. There were cattle still deep in the tide

Aftermath of the storm — Morecambe residents are ferried by the police from their waterlogged homes. (The Visitor, Morecambe)

long after midday. Ewes with their new-born lambs, calves, poultry, hay stacks, mangels, turnips, carts and homes, all were ruined. Only by some miracle the prize beasts had been spared, although they were standing up to their necks in the flood water half a mile from dry land. They could only be approached by boat and this difficult rescue extended well into the afternoon. Almost every farm had suffered, with the loss of its sheep and other animals, and one farmer by the name of Denny lost a valuable horse. On the sea roads, the water was level with the tops of the hedges all day and when eventually it receded the scars of the land crept shuddering into sight. Great holes five and more feet deep, uprooted fencing, railing twisted like cord and everywhere dead things, rabbits, hares, poultry and sheep. The peaceful cared-for country lay broken and horribly disfigured, as if by the riving hands of a malevolent, maddened giant. Today, the farms and sixteen hundred acres of primeval bog, have become modernised and transformed into rich pastures, under the control of the Land Commission.

DANCING
BARS
CAFE

Morecambe will remember the night of 2 January 1976 when the sea crashed through the promenade defences and caused damage amounting to hundreds of thousands of pounds. A repeat of this happened on the night of 15 November 1977, as reported in the newspaper *The Morecambe Visitor*.

The most horrific though spectacular consequence of the storm was the destruction of the West End Pier. It was cut off from the land as the wind and sea swept away a long section, including the Oasis Amusement Arcade, just over an hour after the last bar customers and staff had left. Thick girders and supports were either bent or broken in two by the awesome force of the storm. Shattered arcade walls and roof, and pier decking, were hurled hundreds of yards along the promenade. The full extent of the devastation did not become obvious until daylight on the following day. It was an incredible sight. The pier decking had vanished, leaving behind a grotesque tangle of wood and metal. The whole structure had sagged to one side and collapsed. That Friday night's onslaught, with gusts up to ninety-two miles an hour, flooded more than a thousand homes and business premises in the resort and inflicted severe damage on the sea front. The sea wall was breached at one point between the pier and the stone jetty. Railings were ripped from their foundations and long stretches of the promenade walk were torn up. Several parts of the county town of Lancaster and the surrounding rural areas suffered flooding as well as untold damage. Each new tide brought fears for people over a vast area. Morecambe promenade took the brunt of this nightmare storm, and there were many daring rescues close to the sea front in Morecambe. As the wind continued to blast the town, many of the people who had lost all their possessions gave up the battle against the elements and went to stay with relatives in other parts of the country.

The licensee of the Golden Ball had known many storms during his twenty years' residence in the area. The sea has lapped his railings on a number of occasions when he has had to keep watch during the high tides, but for the first time the sea flooded the lounge and the railings disappeared from view. However, no one was trapped. As the tide continued to rise, the customers were asked to leave for their own safety. Old residents said that such conditions had not been seen since 1905. Again many sheep were drowned along with hundreds of smaller animals. It was a heartbreak awakening for many people as dawn broke over Morecambe, when the full extent of the devastation was revealed. It caused £1,700,000 worth of damage to the resort.

The spectacular storm of November 1977 which destroyed much of Morecambe's West End Pier and caused extensive damage to the resort. The conditions were the worst since 1905. *(The Visitor, Morecambe)*

Soon afterwards, the local authority finalised plans for a £1,800,000 sea wall. This is now partly finished, but on Tuesday, 1 February 1983, Morecambe was hit once again by a nightmare storm, with gusts up to eighty-five miles per hour, which ripped into the resort's defences, taking great chunks out of the sea walls, wrecking promenade shelters, demolishing garden walls, writing off many cars and shattering windows. Several people were hurt. A woman in Marine Road caught the full blast of a window as it blew in, and was taken to hospital with a three inch piece of glass embedded in her side. A young girl received an electric shock when water poured into the basement bathroom at her home as she tried to grab her make-up. Many others were trapped in their basement homes. A number of elderly people marooned on garden walls and shed roofs were hauled to safety in daring rescues as the water swirled past. Once again, it was the people living in basement flats who took the full force of the storm, as in 1977, and again there was a long trail of human misery left in its wake. The many treasured possessions which could be seen floating about on the tide could never be replaced — books, photographs, family treasures such as pictures of the children as babies. They were gone forever.

The areas which were worst hit by the storm were at the north of the promenade. The new wave-reflecting wall helped properties in the East End, although at the height of the storm the tide water was so high that it surged over the top. It was not designed to take the force of such an extra-ordinary force of wind and water that occurred that night. Ironically, the people who suffered most, in the Calton Terrace area, one of the most badly affected places, were next in line for the wave-reflecting wall. Many of the residents agreed that it was far worse than the 1977 floods. Mr. Bob Craine said, "It wasn't just the waves that were coming up, it was just as if the whole sea was here. It's definitely the worst it's ever been, with muddy swirling water creeping slowly up the walls to reach the ceiling." "In 1977," said Mr. Steight, "water was about nine inches deep in the basement. Now it is six or seven feet."

8. Jim Braid of Overton

JUST a little further along the coast-line, below Heysham, is the village of Overton, near the mouth of the river Lune. I travelled down there to see Jim Braid earlier in the summer. He is a hardy character, born of Scottish ancestors who came to settle in Overton. He has been dead keen on fishing from a very early age. I didn't know him personally, but I knew of him and probably he of me, as we are both men of the bay. I took my wife, Olive, with me for the ride, and we reached the village, which I knew fairly well from a visit I made some time ago with my parents. My father had fished with Jim many years ago, in their younger days, so we called at his cottage but unfortunately Jim was out fishing. We were luckier on this later visit. When we pulled up outside the cottage and knocked on the front door, a loud, friendly voice shouted, "Come in."

Jim was so pleased to see us, and as he opened the door he said, "Cu thi-sells in an sit down." "Da-ya-won-a cup-o-tea," and before we had time to say yes or no, he had the kettle on. I told him who I was but I needn't have done. He said "I've sin thee befoor, mi-lad, on't television." Then, "How's them theer lot oor yon side at Fleeakborough?" He asked of several fishermen he had known over the years, and then said, "What is it yer after then?" Well, I was after quite a lot of this man's time, but I was soon assured that this time of the year was the wrong time, as he told me right out. He said, "It's nah good cummin' at this time a year mi-lad. It's aw bed an wark wi us lads, wi'v nah time fer now't else when't salmon's running."

I could see that, although he made us welcome and had shown Olive and me around the cottage, and his magnificently kept allotments, later on in the year he would have more time for us. Judging the man's character, I felt he must have a mine of information in his mind if I hit on the right time. We were so pleased that he had been able to see us, and arranged to come back when work was less plentiful and he would have time and I am sure the pleasure of his reminiscences. I thought to myself, what a remarkable man. Seventy odd years old and as fit as a fiddle. He even showed us how he could touch his toes, and said, "Trouble wi mee-ast folk today is that they eeat-ooer-much and git far ta much sleep. Yan good mee-al a day, does me, an when ah do gah to bed, ah wacken up throught middle ut neet, an think to misel, Oh hell, another fower hours to gah yut!"

After we had arranged to visit him later on in the year, he followed us to the door, and we made off on our journey back home to Grange. Several months passed before I was able to see him again, but I was looking forward to hearing of his experiences, so that when the time came round we set off with great excitement for the village of Overton.

Overton lies on the west side of the river Lune, and was once famous for its boat-building, about two hundred years ago, and there is still a local family engaged in the craft. On meeting up with Jim Braid the second time, he was on his hands and knees in front of the fire with a hand brush. He was sweeping up a few bits of cuttings from a willow basket he had just that minute finished making. Another surprise! He certainly could turn his hand to almost anything.

After the three of us were settled round his cosy fire, he began to tell us of his early days and of how he had bought himself a horse and cart after saving hard. The horse cost him £10 and the cart £1.50 as we would say today. Jim said thirty bob. He then began shrimping and catching plaice and fluke. Later on, he managed to buy a boat for £10 and put a bull-nosed Morris engine in her for trawling. He replaced the boat in 1942 with a much larger one, but unfortunately lost her off Fleetwood in 1957. He himself would certainly have been drowned had it not been for the double-skinned oilskins, which were made at that time. They helped to keep him afloat until he was picked up. The boat was recovered and some time later, whilst coming home from fishing one night, he was knocked over-board when the rail swung round. Again he was lucky; when his brother saw what had happened he came back and picked Jim out of the water.

He was one for the sea and was always thinking of how he could better himself, so he bought a boat at Lytham St Annes and installed in her a diesel engine. He still wasn't satisfied with this type of boat, so he had one built at Whitby, later making a mould from it and built some fibre glass boats for salmon fishing. There will always be plenty of salmon, according to Jim Braid, although he does agree that seasons are shorter with the salmon running much later than they used to do. But, Jim says, they are a later breed.

Up the river Lune, the salmon are trapped and the spawn is squeezed out of them when they are ripe. They are trapped in pens with the water running through constantly, and the pens are divided into suitable sizes. They are so made that the sea-trout can swim through them and up to the top to a pen of their own. Instinct drives them up the river. The same river where they were hatched, perhaps three or four years before.

The eggs are squeezed out when ripe manually into trays. Then, a good cock fish is chosen and the sperm taken from it and put amongst the eggs, and given a good shake-up in a bowl. They are then transferred to a fresh water area, all under cover. A lot of these eggs and the small fry will not live and these have to be picked out with a pair of tweezers. The eggs turn white when they have not been fertilised, and there is one chap who does nothing else but look after the hatchery all the time. Keeping the birds off is one

A fisherman passes under the famous cotton tree at Sunderland Point on the edge of the Lune estuary. Jim Braid of Overton — a little further inland — has many tales of salmon fishing hereabouts. *(T. Parker)*

thing. In the spring of the year the minute salmon are turned out into the river where they stay for two years. If one jumps nearby, you will see a thousand jump altogether, just like raindrops. At two years old they are about five inches in length and they go down the river then, and keep going. Here one day, seen jumping, and gone the next. They swim out of the river and away to the Arctic circle and here they feed under the ice.

If there are some early developers among this batch of salmon, these make their way back to the same river as three year olds. If they have any spawn in them they have to find fresh water. "They come to the surface and swim like hell," as Jim says, wanting to get back to spawn. Most salmon though wait until they are four years old and then come back in a huge mass. "An' if there's any late developers in this lot, them's um which is the big uns, twenty pounders." Jim tells me he once got a forty-two pounder, the biggest he has ever caught, but his father once caught one which weighed in at fifty one and a half pounds. "It's not often ya catch any o'them soo-ert nowadays."

The river Lune has silted up over the years, and there are no good deep holes for the fish to lie in, so lave netting is nothing like as good as it used to be.

Wamaling is a very specialist mode of fishing — not for the inexperienced. An open boat with an engine is used, and a wamal net of about 320 yards. The most important though is the know-how of the professional fisherman. They usually fish alone. He would shoot the net at about three and a half hours' ebb from Sunderland Breast, and drift down to the mouth of the river Lune, shooting and hauling as he went. The fishermen are out for seven hours each tide and this means fourteen hours out of the twenty-four. Knowledge of every little bank and channel is essential if the salmon are to be caught.

If it wasn't for the inshore fishermen, there would be far more fatalities in the bay. Jim remembers when he was coming home from shrimping one night, seeing two policemen angling from a small boat. It was blowing half a gale at the time and Jim was sailing up the south side of the Lune. These chaps seemed to be in a spot of bother, so Jim said to his brother, "I'se guyn back for them fellahs, thur in trouble." But his brother replied, "Nay, wur nut guyn back, we've gitten enough of our arn troubles, wi-out anybody else's." Jim took no notice of this and turned the boat round and made over to the two policemen. He drew alongside, pulled their anchor up and took them in tow up the river towards home. But said Jim, "I needn't a bothered wi one of um, poor chap deed 'of an 'eart attack the following day." The man had been so terrified that he was actually frightened to death, and fear can kill.

The next rescue, with a happier ending, occurred one May. There weren't many salmon about, so Jim thought he would try trawling, but his shrimp-beam was up under the shore at Overton. It was a thick fog at the time, but after collecting the beam and sailing down the river, the fog lifted a bit, just as if it had to at that time, otherwise he would not have been able to see something black on the top of what looked like a bridge to Sunderland. He couldn't make out what this object could be, and thought it was "damned queer," so he sailed away out into the river and back up this gutter, and found a fellow kneeling down in water on the top of a van, which was under the tide — an exceptionally high one at that time of the year. Knowing that so often anyone in trouble will try to come towards his rescuer, even if quite a distance away, Jim shouted to him, "Don't move whatever tha does. I'll be wi yah in a tick." This rescue wasn't straightforward, as Jim had to sail and manoeuvre his boat between the bridge and the submerged van, and had difficult moments. As the tide swirled over the bridge, it took Jim's boat in the wrong direction, but after several attempts he rammed the boat right in and he made it to the stranded man. He was an elderly chap and after the rescue, Jim took him to the nearest place which was Sunderland.

Jim never carries a compass and tells me he smells his way around. The man he saved was travelling to Sunderland over the low marsh road, and this does get covered with reasonably high tide. Luckily, he was on the highest part of the bridge, otherwise he would probably have been drowned.

Following this, Jim went to play bingo at Morecambe football club and he began to chat with the man at the next table. "Where do you come from then?" the fellow asked. "Overton," said Jim. "Oh," said the chap, "We used to come down to Overton and go to Sunderland Point, but we've never bin lately. Eye, mi' father had a queer do once down theer. He got stuck in't tide. Da ya know any fishermen about theer?" Jim said, "I nah em aw" meaning "I know them all." "Well," the chap said, "Dad was lucky. Fog was so thick that no one could a seen him from any wheer, and if it'd not bin fer that fisherman, dad would a bin drowned." He said again, "So yah know 'em aw, do yah?" "Well," said Jim, "I nah that yan, it wer me." Amazed, the fellow said, "Well I nivver. What are yah drinking?" All Jim said was, "I don't drink."

Over the years Jim has helped to save many lives and he has also had the experience of picking bodies up from the sands. As a lad of fourteen years, he had his first such experience when he found the body of a Bradford woman. He took her to the mortuary in a milk-float and passed through the village of Overton. He had covered the body with a sheet, but with the jolting of the cart, every now and then her hand would pop out of the covering, but Jim said, "I wasn't freekened of 'er." Even today, he can remember that she had a white handkerchief in her hand, and in the corner was embroidered her name "Martha" in blue silk. He can see that in his mind even after all these years.

Such another was whilst going out fishing one day with his brother and they could see a lump or object out on the sands. His brother Dick said, "Gah en luck yonder an see wot it is." Jim said, "Nah thee gah," but said Dick, "Ise nut guyn to be chessed wi a body, bugger you." So Jim went over to see and came back to his brother who asked, "Well is it a body?" Jim replied, "Ah doant nah." Over the years Jim has picked up many a body and sometimes he has been taken in by a tailor's dummy! This body had been in the water for some time, and had changed colour. It was a woman who had been drowned off Fleetwood about ten days before, so they left her and went to inform the police. "Ey Braid, you're not having us on a wild goose chase, with one of your dummies, are you?" Said Jim, "Look 'ere mate, I've picked up bodies off these sands afore tha was born," feeling very annoyed with the inspector. It is said that it takes nine days for a body to float to the top after being drowned in salt water, unless of course it is carried onto a sandbank much earlier.

Finishing on a happier note, I found that in Jim's younger days he was very musical. He played the piano and the piano-accordion, and often used to play to his pals. He still has his accordion but he cannot play now, as his fingers are too stiff.

Spartina grass — which has established itself on sand near the shoreline.

9.   Walney Island

ACROSS the bay at Walney Island, in 1790 a lighthouse was to be built, and a charter was granted to the Port of Lancaster Commissioners for the building of it. This was built, lit and inspected from the sea by 1791. The soft white sandstone of which it was built was ferried from a quarry owned by the commission at Overton, near Lancaster. It was taken in flat-bottomed barges towed by schooners and landed near the site.

When visibility permitted, I had seen the flashing light across the bay when out doing my fishing at night, but I had never been near to the lighthouse on Walney and thought it would be of interest, so I decided to have a ride through one day and take my wife Olive with me. We enquired the way once we reached Walney, and soon we were leaving the built up areas and found ourselves going down a long bumpy lane, full of pot-holes. We pulled up at a farm and enquired whether we were on the right road. We were assured that we were going in the right direction, and as long as we had permission or had been in touch with the lighthouse keeper, the farmer said we should be alright. "She can be a bit of a queer old stick, but she'll 'appen be alreet wi you, when you tell 'er wot you want." Well, we drove on and on, not knowing what to expect. Eventually, we came alongside the lighthouse and all seemed very quiet, apart from the squawking of the seagulls. I got out of the car and said to Olive, "You had better stay here, you never know what is going to greet us." I knocked on a door and very soon a chap came out and asked what I was after. I told him who I was and where I was from and that I would like to see the lighthouse keeper. "Wait a minute," he said, "I'll see if I can find her." Before long he came back saying she was doing a bit of gardening but would see us in a minute. We both waited anxiously to see if we would be accepted or whether we should be sent on our way. As the lighthouse keeper came towards us she had a smile on her face. I thought she is not going to be as bad as she's made out to be. I told her I would be interested to know a little bit about the lighthouse, and asked whether she could spare a few minutes to talk to us. She was very polite and asked us in for a cup of tea and a biscuit. We enjoyed her company very much and the information she gave us was most interesting. Mrs. Peggy Braithwaite, the lady we were speaking to, is the only woman lighthouse keeper in Britain, and has lived at the lighthouse for most of her life. She became principal keeper about eight years ago, following in her father's footsteps.

The cost of building the lighthouse was £1,500 and it was completed in twelve months. It is approximately 75 feet high and there are 91 steps up the inside. These form part of the outer wall and the inside column. Originally it was lit with soft-wick lamps filled with seal or whale oil, which had to be warmed over a charcoal stove in cold weather, so that the wicks could soak it up. The charcoal stove which was used in those far off days is now in the Museum of Lancaster. Following several modifications in 1953, the lamp was lit by generated electricity and in 1970 it went on to the national grid.

Ships were always in grave danger when sailing around the Lancashire coast before the days of the lighthouse. Shipwrecks were too numerous to mention. Even after the lighthouse was built, there were still many recordings of vessels wrecked off Walney Island. In 1862 a sailing ship carrying red flannel from Lancashire mills to India came ashore at Hillock Whins and nearly all the population of Biggar, Walney, turned out and everyone on the island had red flannel underwear, bed clothes and curtains for a long time afterwards. An Irish potato boat came ashore at Biggar Bank. Tommy Gilliland had the job of carting the potatoes off. Some vessels of the Spanish Armada were wrecked off Walney Island and relics are reported to be on show in Brown's Museum in Liverpool.

On 14 July 1901, off South Walney during a gale, a vessel loaded with coal for Mr. Robert Robinson of Ulverston got into difficulties. The crew were

The lighthouse at the southern tip of Walney Island. *(W. R. Mitchell)*

rescued by Joe Kendal and friends who pulled them through the surf by rope. Previously at the same spot, a sloop, the *Aurora* of about thirty tons was wrecked. This was in 1825 but unfortunately her crew perished being washed ashore. They all belonged to Preston, Lancashire. One of them had 36 gold sovereigns and vessel papers on him, and another had a watch.

The Commers of 70 tons was lying off Rampside three miles south-east of Barrow on 23 March 1827 with two hundred barrels of gunpowder which blew up without warning. The explosion was heard and felt as far away as Lancaster and Preston and the damage great.

In the churchyard on Walney Island are the graves of the crew of the brig *Susan*, wrecked on 6 November 1825. Her master was John Welsh, 44 years of age, another victim of the treacherous seas on this coast. The captain's wife asked for the money belt which her husband always carried, but it could not be found. Later it was found stuffed down a rabbit hole. The bodies of the crew of the stricken ship had been laid in a barn at Biggar village. The barn was at a later date said to be haunted by the captain who became well-known as the "South End Dobbie".

Mrs. Wild of North Scale told me of how ships were lured ashore in the early days by false lights. A lantern was fixed to the head of a donkey and as the animal moved about the light seemed to signal to ships in the area and they would run aground and were looted. Mrs. Wild's grandfather told her of how one Sunday morning at church (and the church was always well attended in those days), first one man would slip outside quietly and then another then others one by one would go. There would be whispering going round the congregation and then the vicar took off his surplice and said, "Wait for me — hang on lads — we may as well all get some." And away they went, leaving the church to look after itself. Their object was the cargo of a ship which had been wrecked.

Another tale was of a man who lived in the village. He was very fond of his ale, but greatly disliked newcomers in the village. He was known for his summing up of these people and said, "I don't know, they're ignorant buggers . . . bin now-where, seen nowt . . . know nowt. They only know three things. East side of Walney, green fields and cow shite."

Walney Island is nine miles long but not more than a mile wide. One hundred years ago the population was just over two hundred but since then has increased by leaps and bounds. It is reached by a bridge from Barrow-in-Furness. The south end of the island has a very large gullery and some rare flowers. Eiderduck also come to nest there.

An interesting character who has a few tales to tell is Bob Benson, who was bred and born on the island, as were his father and grandfather also. Going back many years, there was a road-sweeper in Biggar village by the name of Tom Kendal. He was a big man and quite a character. He was sitting breaking stones to make material for road making, when he saw a rabbit pop out of the hedgerow. He said to Bob's grandfather, "I decided I would have it." At dinner time he came back with his eight bore shot gun, which was a muzzle loader and he put six drams of gunpowder and two ounces of shot in it, but bunny never came out again that day. The following morning he took the gun along with him. In his own words he said, "I was sitting there cracking my stones when out come bunny. I picked up my gun and let fly. When I came to, the gun was in the hedge, the rabbit was without it's head, and I had a damn sore jaw." He had forgotten the gun was loaded, and had put another six drams of gunpowder and a further loading of shot. It must have been a very well-made gun to stand that lot! And it must have been Tom's lucky day.

Then there was Riley from Biggar. He found an old wooden horse trough washed up on the tideline. He was a young lad at the time, but he made a boat out of it and used it for long enough. The same chap later got married and at the time he had some nets set near to Sheep Island. He used to go out to look to the nets on a motor-cycle combination. One night the cycle got stuck in the sands and he ran all the way back to Biggar for his wife and between them they managed to dig it out before the tide turned. Can you imagine any women of today who would have gone out onto the sands on a wild, wet night to dig out a motor-cycle combination, when she had only been married a week!

At the village of North Scale there is a footbridge. It can be used at low tide to cross to the mainland. In former days the bridge was used almost every day, as there was no public transport and Walney Bridge was a toll bridge. At low water there is about a foot or so of water round the footbridge. One night, Bob overheard two wollies talking, and it went like this, "When you come over the bridge at night Frank, and you have had a skinful, you want to walk alongside it. You only get wet up to your knees, whereas if you fall off it you get wet all over." Frank said, "That is a good idea of yours, Charlie, I will try it next time." And he did!

The north end of Walney Island was a lot different in those far off days. Only the small village, no housing estate as there is today. When Bob was a lad, he couldn't understand why families on the island seemed to have plenty of cash, yet never worked as such. Bob asked his grandfather, Captain Benson, where they got their money from. He said they were all the descendants of wreckers, who lured ships ashore with false lights, and then plundered their cargo of grain, coal or whatever the ship might be carrying. One such person kept the inn and had money of his own. Apart from the wreckers, most people worked on the land and were only paid once a quarter. When they had spent the coin of the realm in which they were paid, the landlady of the inn would give them tokens, which had the same face value. They would pay for their ale with these tokens, and then at term end would pay up with the real stuff.

One of the best known sons of North Scale was the late Ambrose Turner. He was a great person and one of nature's gentlemen. Ambrose earned his

Tight-rope act on the Walney Island stakes — driven into much of the shoreline in an attempt to reduce erosion. *(T. Parker)*

living from fishing and guthenny — a weed of the rocks. It is a wet, cold job gathering it in wintertime, but he was a very hardy soul.

Bob's other pals were Artie Sharp, Joe Ayres, Vernon Littlewood and one or two others. Sadly, most of them have now passed on, except for Bob and Walter Knowles. Some died in foreign lands while fighting for their country but Bob sincerely believes that Ambrose died of a broken heart when he saw what they had done to his island. The housing estate was the last straw.

A short distance away is Piel Island, and Frank Moore carried on many of the traditions of the island. When he left school at fourteen years of age he did a bit of fishing with his father. He did some ferrying too. At sixteen years, he started work on the pilot boat at Barrow, and was skipper-engineer of the old Barrow-Heysham pilot boats for seventeen years. Then, in 1954, he took over the lifeboat job when his father retired. He also carried on the business of the Post Office on Roa Island, taking the post over to Piel by rowing boat which had long been the tradition also.

Frank's father often told the tale of when he himself was a lad of about ten years old and his pal Fred would go to the castle on Piel Island and sit by the wall, having a crafty smoke and seeing who could say the most swear words.

He had heard the tale of the Black Abbot of Piel and had told the tale to Fred. They thought nothing about it, until this particular day, when looking towards an open window the figure of the ghost passed by. They left in such a hurry that their feet seemed never to touch the ground, and needless to say they never went back to the castle again. Frank's father swore to his dying day that he had seen the ghost of the Black Abbot of Piel Island.

Frank Moore remembers as a lad among lads on the island, there was very little schooling, for they had to rely on the weather being good enough to make it possible for old Tommy Swarbrick to row the youngsters across to Roa Island where they would attend school. More often than not they would get there about eight-thirty in the morning, and maybe an hour or so later, Tommy would be back saying, "We'll have to be getting back now, I's not coming back again for you lot today." So of course, they would all go home, and this suited the children.

On the island of Piel is the Old Castle which dates back to the early thirteen hundreds. The monks came to Furness in the year 1127 and cultivated much of the area. As for the Black Abbot, whether he has at last found rest, or is still haunting the ruins of the castle, no one knows. On the island there is also a pub called the Ship Inn. At one time the island was well inhabited, and there was a row of cottages where all the pilots, ferrymen and fishermen lived, but when houses were built on Roa Island the pilots moved across into them.

The island people were very hardy characters in those days. Between the south end of Walney and Piel Island there is a stretch of water, but at low water this dries out and it is possible to walk across from one to the other. The Barrow channel runs between Piel and Roa islands, and Frank's grandfather used to row to and from work at the shipyard. Sometimes, he would walk across the sands, depending on the weather. Frank's grandfather lived and died by the sea. He was going across the sands to Walney, and got cut off by the tide and was drowned. He wasn't the only one, as there have been several drownings over the years. The tide comes through the meetings and soon becomes a raging sea.

Roa Island used to be an island years ago, until the causeway was built by the Furness Railway. This was when cattle were brought over from Ireland, and were then herded into wagons and brought down the branch line to Barrow. At one time practically all the cattle came via Roa Island.

The Ship Inn in Piel Island used to belong to the Duke of Buccleugh many years ago, until he found it to be a liability to him, so he gave it to Barrow Corporation. The land was to be used as a recreation ground. The inn is now rented out, and the grazing right and anything the landlord can muster goes with it. The acreage is between thirty to forty acres, and usually farmers from Ulpha area bring their sheep down to graze on the island in wintertime. Today beer is taken across to the island by tractor and trailer when the tide is out. Years ago it was taken by boat, and the crates of beer had to be carried up the pier to the inn. Customers often came in by the sea during the summertime, and at weekends yachts from Fleetwood and Glasson Dock sail over to the island. They anchor up and the passengers go ashore and spend the evenings in the pub, and some of them stay overnight. The pub is only manned in the summertime, but at one time the landlord had to be there all the time, according to his lease.

During the war years the only person living on the island was Mrs. Martin who kept the pub. There was no ferry and no boating as there is today. She must have had a very lonely life. Her husband was lost at sea, after Frank's father got him the job on a coaster. The first trip out the ship was torpedoed. Two or three months after his ship had been lost, his wife discovered a body washed up right alongside the pier at Piel Island on the highwater mark. She looked at the body but as there was no post or other communication then, time went by without her seeing a soul and the body just lay there for a week. She kept going out to take another look at the body and when Frank and his father went over one day, she came down to the pier and met them, and said to them, "Hey! There's a body washed up near the top end of the pier. It's been there several days now." Frank and his father went back and told the police, who went over and collected the body. Mrs. Martin said afterwards, "I'm bliddy sure that was Bert's body." Bert was her husband. She said, "I've had another look at it and I knitted him a pair of socks just like the ones on that body, the very same pattern." She never claimed the body as her husband's, but wished afterwards that she had done and then given him a decent burial. Of course, the body was hardly recognisable by its features, as it had been in the water for quite some time.

Mrs. Martin was certainly a character, and as sturdy as an ox. When the two men took coal over to the island by boat, Frank would carry the heavy sacks up the pier. She would say, "Oh, leave it there, just drop it and I'll take it away a bit at a time", and she would pick up a hundred-weight sack of coal and put it in a wheelbarrow and away she would go with it, with no effort at all. Frank's father used to say, "I'm bliddy sure she's got one knacker", meaning she was half a man.

Many years before this, she had a son living with her on the island. He got very little schooling and with seeing no one he was almost wild. When anyone did go over to the island, he would run around the back of the pub, climb onto the roof, hide behind the chimney stack and wait until the person had gone before he would come down again. At sixteen years of age, he left the island and went to sea, and became one of the best men on the ship. This was said of him wherever he went.

As seafaring men, Frank and his father were always at the ready when assistance was needed out in the bay. During the war in 1943 in the blackout there was a fishing boat with two fellows aboard; it had dragged its anchor in a south-westerly gale. The lifeboat's boarding boat was launched on a pitch black night at 10 pm. Not a light could be seen anywhere, and this boat was only about three hundred yards from the lifeboat slip just before high water. And the sea! Well it was hellish rough. Frank and his father had made three attempts at launching the dinghy before they could get clear of the shore, as the fierce waves washed it back, time after time. At last, they were on their way and rowed off into the night bringing the two men back safely to the shore. Just ten minutes afterwards, the boat from which they had rescued the two men came drifting alongside the lifeboat pier, where it hit once or twice and knocked a hole in its side and sank straight to the bottom. It must have been about a month later when they heard that they had been awarded a bronze medal apiece for their brave rescue.

In 1958 while out shooting with a friend, Frank saw a flare from the Morecambe Bay lightship. A man had been taken ill with appendicitis, and the lightship was moored sixteen miles out from Walney in Morecambe Bay. Trinity House had their own big tender that used to come round from time to time and they decided they would have to take the sick man ashore. The weather was really rough. Not fit to turn man and boat out, so it was decided to leave it until the following day to see if had moderated. Well, the morrow came and it was still blowing a gale. "Oh well, we can't do anything in this weather, if the man is no worse, we'll see what it is like tomorrow." These were the thoughts of the would be rescuers. That was on a Wednesday. It was still blowing a gale. At seven o'clock on Wednesday evening Frank's brother, who was coxwain of the Barrow lifeboat, came round to Frank's house and said, "Are you coming for a sail?" Frank said, "What for?" "Oh we've been called out to Morecambe Bay Lightship, to bring this 'ere fella back ashore." So off they went and gathered the crew and launched. It was only sixteen miles, but it took them more than three hours to get out there. The lifeboat was rearing up and pounding down on the wild seas. Mountainous high was Frank's description. Rearing up . . . and pounding down, but it eased up a little once they got off into the deeper water. Eventually they reached the vessel and got the fellow off.

The coxwain said to Frank, "What da ya think about goin' home again?" "Well," said Frank, "that's all I've been thinking about all the way out here." Frank explained to me that when you are running with a following sea, that's where the danger lies of broaching to and capsizing. The huge waves coming up behind pick the boat up and control is lost to the mercy of the sea. This was already a dangerous mission, but would have been more so had they returned the way they had come. A discussion went on and a decision was made fairly quickly. Had they to go in at Fleetwood? But this would have been very much the same. Then Frank said, "How about going in at the Isle of Man?" The coxwain didn't like that idea, as he thought there might be a strong north-westerly wind flying out from that direction. In those days they had no chart of Morecambe Bay, so the coxwain told Frank to call the Liverpool Pilot boat on the radio and ask him for a course and distance from Morecambe Bay light-vessel to Liner's Point, Anglesey. They were

The lonely sea and the sky. A solitary individual gazes out towards the setting sun from Walney's western shore. *(Leslie Sansom)*

given a course and the distance was forty-five miles. They set off on that course and kept the lifeboat head-on to the mountainous seas. They were in no real danger, as long as they could keep it on that course, steaming into the huge waves and down the other side. They left the lightship at eleven o'clock that night and didn't reach Mulborough in Anglesey until five the next morning. When they pulled alongside the lifeboat pier there and opened the engine-room hatch to stop the engine, they found it half full of water. "Oh hell," said Frank, "What's up now?" They got on the phone to head office, and their advice was to take the boat down to Beaumaris and get it slipped — that is, put on the slipway to find out what the trouble was. On inspection, they found there were some bilge pieces hanging off, no doubt caused by the pounding the boat had taken in the rough seas on their perilous voyage. The three-quarter inch bolts they were fastened on with were bent and the holes through which the bolts were fastened were worn to an oval shape, so great had been the stress and strain on the boat. Owing to the amount of damage, the boat was there from September until January. The coxwain received a bronze medal for the trip some time later.

The crew then had to make their way home by train, and when they were leaving the coxwain told the men to fetch the two bottles of rum which they always carried. It was neat rum, good stuff. They also carried a supply of chocolate, but it was the rum that the coxwain was worried about. "We're not leaving it for them blighters in the boatyard, they'll only sup it," he said. So it was taken with them, and as they left the yard they all went into this pub at Mulborough. One of the crew had the two bottles hidden under his coat. He pulled them out and said to the barman, "Can you pull the corks out of these for us?" Fancy going into a pub to drink their own rum! Mind you, that was typical of Norman. They all had a good laugh afterwards.

Six years ago Frank Moore was awarded the B.E.M. in the New Year's honours list. He has been with the lifeboat since 1937 and has served a total of forty-seven years. He has never really known fear all these years, not until he gets back home. Then he has time to sit and think of what could have happened.

The lifeboat *Herbert Leigh* was named after a paint manufacturer from Bolton. He had connections with Vickers of Barrow in Furness, where he sold his paints and marine parts. He always wanted to buy a lifeboat, but said he could never afford it, but in 1951 he finally had the money to buy one. He said to the Lifeboat Institution that he wanted it stationed on the Lancashire coast. Just at that time, Barrow was due for a replacement, so it came to Barrow. It cost him £25,000 but when it went for a complete overhaul, with new engines etc, it cost £26,000. Nowadays, the lifeboats which are being built cost £300,000.

10. Natural History

MORECAMBE BAY is an outstanding habitat for wild birds and it is impossible to imagine what it would be like without them. All the year round they are with us, but in wintertime the bay becomes host to thousands of waders — as many as 100,000 may make it their winter feeding ground. With their specialised beaks, some long, some short, others straight, or curved up or down, they probe the mud and sand, for the juicy morsels which dwell beneath.

Between tides, the birds move ceaselessly, searching for food. At low water, 120 square miles of sand and mud are exposed and, as the tide recedes, the thousands of birds, waders, wildfowl, gulls and terns, are drawn by the abundance of food so readily available. The sheltered shores and islands also provide safe nesting places for many of the birds from April to June. Then all the bird life is at its peak, for courtship, nest building and rearing of the family. The plumage is brighter than at any other time.

There is no mistaking the curlew, typical of the moors in spring and summer, but in winter curlews flock to the coastal mud-flats of the bay to feed. It is the largest of the wading birds and is easily recognised by its brown streaked plumage, long, down-curved bill and familiar whistling call. Being a shy bird, the curlew is very wary and flies off at the first sign of danger.

The most common of the large waders to be seen in the bay is the oystercatcher, called by the local people "sea-a-pie," with its black and white plumage and its orange bill. It is one of the most vociferous of the waders, and their incessant babbling can be heard wherever a group of them is feeding. Even on a dark night, the fishermen can locate the cockle beds by the endless babble of the "sea-a-pies." Their food consists of a wider variety than most of the waders, though cockles are their favourite food. Oystercatchers also feed on mussels and can often be seen on the mussel beds off Morecambe, Heysham, Rampside and Knott End and Fleetwood. Large beds of the common mussel are found on the stony scars in these areas. Young mussels, called spat, settle on the scars during the late winter and early spring, but the numbers of these are greatly reduced by the many smaller birds, the knot, dunlin, and others.

At one time, it was believed that there were so many oystercatchers that they were taking more cockles in the day than the fishermen. In fact, thousands of these birds were killed for this reason on the Welsh coast, but nature soon restored the balance, and in a hard winter such as the 1962/63

Oystercatchers — locally known as "Sea-a-pies" — facing the wind.

winter, the oystercatchers along with other birds were driven off the shore inland in search of food, finding earth worms a good substitute for the cockles which had been killed off by the severe frosts.

Another very widespread and abundant source of food is the hen-penny (Macoma bathica), a delicate pink-coloured shellfish, and although it can grow up to one inch in length, most specimens in Morecambe Bay are much smaller, and many species of wader feed on these as do the flatfish.

The tide runs into the bay twice in twenty-four hours, with one week of low tides (neap tides) followed by a week of high tides. On the neaps, acre upon acre of high level sand flats are never reached by the tide for several days. These flats dry out considerably, and in such areas, as along the coastline at Grange over Sands, many different species of wader can be observed feeding closely together on the slightly lower areas which have remained waterlogged. On the dry areas, the invertebrates retreat further under the surface into the moisture of the lower levels, limiting the feedng grounds until the tide rises, covering the whole area of the bay and lapping at the embankments and shoreline around the coasts.

An estuary is up to three times more fertile than the best farmland, with nutrients being obtained from the rivers and the sea. The high tides contribute to the erosion around our coasts, but the growth increase is mainly due to the sediment brought down the rivers, and secondly to eroded material from adjoining coasts. The gains are chiefly in tidal estuaries and the losses on the open coasts, but the largest gains around the whole of the British coast are Morecambe Bay, Southport and the Wash.

Nothing perhaps looks so barren of life as a big stretch of sand at low tide, and only the man out to dig lug worms or sand eels would find out for himself just what lies beneath the sand. There are tell-tale marks which spell out to the experienced person just what creatures abound in that area.

A sand-hopper (corophium volutator) lives in U-shaped burrows on less exposed shores of the bay. A little khaki-coloured creature, it is up to one third of an inch long. It scuttles round and round in half circles but sometimes takes amazing leaps. When large numbers are together, they make quite a hissing sound, and they can be a nuisance to people during the summer-time, whilst having a picnic on the marshes, as they find their way into teacups, the picnic basket and everywhere else. Luckily, they are eaten in large numbers by the dunlin, redshank, ringed plover and the sanderling.

A small marine snail (Hydrobia ulvae), which is plentiful on many sandbanks, is dark, and when present in large numbers the surface of the sand looks granular.

Over the last few years I have been lucky in being asked to take a group of students from Bradford University out into the bay on my tractor and trailer, to dig in the sands and then take their findings back safely in containers for study — a kind of marine biology. We would set out from the shore to arrive at a point furthest away, around low water mark. Then the students would be eager to make a start with their buckets and spades. This was all new to me and I was seeing things which I had not even noticed before in all my life out on the bay. We would work over a large area, then move on, perhaps half a mile or so towards home, then stop again probably near some sand which looked slightly different. Each stop was educational, not only to the students but also to me.

The marine snail (Hydrobia ulvae) was the most interesting to me, as a sample area of sand was marked out for studies. A cut with a spade, carefully, about nine inches to a foot depth, brought to the surface something which is really remarkable to look at. The sand is tunnelled in all directions, like a network of railway junctions, and in these the busy little creature, the marine snail, was so prolific that no tropical jungle could compare with the sands for sheer mass production.

Birds of Morecambe Bay. Top left: Common Tern. Top right: Lesser Black-backed Gull. Bottom left: Curlew. Bottom right: Lapwing — or Pewit.

The lapwing, also known as the pewit or tewit, can be seen picking its way over ploughed fields on the salt marshes and prodding about in the estuary mud. It is a strikingly colourful bird with a curious tuft of feathers on its head. In group flights they are noticeable as they wheel and turn showing off their skills. The colours of the bird, black and white with green shades on the back and brilliant white on the underside, are brought out on a clear day with the sunlight to great advantage.

Bird life is abundant in the bay and on the marshes, and the many differing species of gull can be seen from the shore. The common tern resembles the gull but is smaller and more graceful. It is grey and white with a noticeably forked tail. They come to the bay in April and stay until October. They build a very sparse nest of marine and vegetable matter on the sandy flats of the marshes and lay two or three buff-coloured eggs. The nests are dotted about the marsh fairly close together and the birds rely on small fish for their diet.

Although in my daily travels across the sands of the bay I see almost every species of wild bird, surprisingly they don't take flight at the first sight and sound of my old tractor. They must have become accustomed to it and know they will come to no harm as I pass large numbers of shellduck and mallard at close range. My favourite bird of the bay is the heron, and although they are found all around the bay, over the past two years I have seen as many as nine of these majestic birds standing not so far out on the sands from the Kents Bank area. The herons seemed more aware of other birds, mainly of the gulls, than the noise of the tractor. No one in the ordinary way of life would be able to get as near to the birds of the bay as I do but as I go about my job of fishing for flukes regularly, I am lucky. There is always a lot of waste from the filleting, and the heads and guts are taken back to the sands and thrown out for the birds to clean up. They soon learn that the tractor means there is a meal for them and they can be seen in large flocks — mostly gulls — at the self-same spot as on the previous day. I notice the heron seems to shy away from the gulls, and doesn't attempt to go near, standing well back until the gulls have had their fill. I tried tipping the waste into several heaps to see if I could encourage the herons to have a good feed, but no, they would only approach the food after the gulls had had their fill and had left the area. After a while, it was pleasing to see on my homeward journey from the sands that several of the herons were tucking into the fluke remains. The heron is easily recognised by its long neck and legs, grey back and white head and underparts streaked with black. It stands motionless in shallow water, waiting for the fish and eels to swim within reach, then with a swift movement the luckless prey is snapped up by the long beak and quickly swallowed.

Popular with visitors is the Leighton Moss Nature Reserve at Silverdale, and the new education centre is most impressive. The old building on the site became derelict, and although plans were in the air to develop them for a recreation and education centre, nothing was done owing to lack of money. Then the folks from the Countryside Commission gave a grant for the development. The conversion took about two years, but now the very fine building is in use. There is a wonderful display of pictures on the first floor, showing the many and various habitats to be found in the vast area covered by Leighton Moss, Morecambe Bay and the whole of Arnside. It is a great attraction, and shows the natural history of this wide area. There are so many different things to see, from the limestone pavements, considerable woodland and the fen which they have at Leighton, along with the salt marshes and the sand flats of Morecambe Bay. This display takes one through these habitats and gives a view of what can be seen throughout the year. It also shows the importance of these particular habitats for nature conservation.

The highlight of an afternoon's visit would be the sighting of the bearded tit. It is the only place in the north-west of England where they nest. Besides the birds, there are many interesting plants which can be seen while walking around, and this is nature as its best. Everyone will learn something worthwhile and will be that much wiser for their visit to this interesting part of our country.

On a typical Sunday four to five hundred people arrive at the centre and maybe a hundred of them will make a tour of the reserve. They can see teal, mallard, tufted ducks and goldeneye, among many others, and the smaller birds such as the bearded tits can be heard calling. Hundreds of starlings fly in late in the afternoon, coming in to roost in the reed beds. To see the huge flocks of starlings swirling then circling and twisting in the air is one of nature's most exciting sights in the autumn countryside.

Leighton Moss lies close to the north-east tip of Morecambe, between Silverdale and Yealand Redmayne, and the reserve occupies 321 acres of unspoilt and attractively wooded valley flanked by limestone hills. One of the special features is the extensive reed beds. They have been an R.S.P.B. reserve since 1964 when they were leased from Major and Mrs. Reynolds of Leighton Hall. Finally, the reserve was purchased by the R.S.P.B. in 1974.

Over the other side of the bay, on the west coast close to Barrow-in-Furness, lies the South Walney Nature Reserve, managed by the Cumbria Trust for Nature Conservation for the owners Holker Estates. This island has been the breeding ground for sea-birds for centuries. The majority of the reserve is the breeding ground of two of the most common European sea-birds, the herring gull and the lesser black-backed gull. From a few pairs nesting here in the 1920s, the population has grown into about 49,000 breeding pairs, with equal numbers of each species. The herring gull is non-migratory, and during the winter months it remains in or near the reserve, though a few individuals do go into north-western Europe. Although the major part of the reserve is occupied by gulls, over 150 other species have been seen since it opened. The distribution of the birds at breeding time is of considerable interest, but a permit is necessary to visit the reserve and this must be obtained from the Warden, Coastguard Cottages, South Walney, Barrow-in-Furness, Cumbria, (Tel: 0229 41066), either in advance or immediately on arrival. Group permits must always be obtained in advance.

The reserve is open throughout the year from 10 a.m. but is closed on Mondays except on Bank Holiday Monday. Visitors must be off the reserve by 7 p.m. during the months of May to August inclusive, and no entry is allowed after 5 p.m. From September to April inclusive visitors must be off the reserve by 4 p.m. The reserve is approached from Barrow-in-Furness by crossing the bridge and turning left at the traffic lights at the Walney end of the bridge. Then follow the promenade and Ocean Road which swings right at the King Alfred Hotel. The fourth road on the left, Carr Lane, continues for a good five miles; the last couple of miles is unmetalled and is over private land. The visitor must keep to the road, drive at a speed not exceeding fifteen miles an hour, and must pass through without stopping. The best time to see eggs and chicks is late May, the whole of June and early July.

Now let us make our way to the sea shore. Very little was once written about seashore life, but now that has all changed. Our coastal waters are nurseries for small fish, flukes, plaice, shrimps, crabs and so forth, all living within the tidal area. Although our waters are chilly compared with a coral reef, they are crowded enough with life of all kinds, and it is impossible for me to deal with them all, so let us follow the tide out of this ever-changing bay.

Stones brought down by the river waters, and masses of rock which has fallen from the cliffs, have been rolled by the action of the tide into smooth pebbles, often strewn along the coastline, and it is worth while taking a close look as many interesting fossils can be found. The Grange over Sands area is particularly rich and is well-known to fossil hunters.

On a sandy shore there is an abundance of animal life. When the sea fisheries officer is engaged on taking a census of seashore, he takes a sample of sand and mud and by counting all the living creatures it contains he can assess with reasonable accuracy the population of a whole beach. On some parts of our shores the figures are staggering. For instance, the common lug worm may lie as many as eighty thousand to the acre! Everyone at some time has been on the sands and noticed little piles of worm castings. Each pile marks the tailend of a worm. The worm rests in a U shape below the sand, its mouth being just below a round dent which is always an inch or two away from the squiggly pile of castings. The cast marks the sand which has passed through the worm's inside.

The lug worm (Corophium Volutator) is buried in U-shaped tunnels under the sand and leaves its casts on the surface.

The greater number of the sand dwellers use the sand as a place of refuge, and lie buried in it securely hidden from foes, although some of these creatures give themselves away by advertising their presence as plainly as does the lug worm. Buried in the sand is the gaper clam, with a kind of keyhole mark on the surface. If we were to dig well down in the sand, we would find this big shellfish hinged like a mussel, and with a dark-coloured drain barrel sticking out at one end. This drainpipe also gives away the secret of how nearly all the sand burrowers can spend so much time buried alive without being suffocated. All of them must have some means of reaching the water above, and they do this by a tube-like structure as do the clams.

Another class of sea worm uses the sand for building purposes and there are scores of these tube-building worms around our shores. To the ordinary seaside visitor, most of the worms only reveal their whereabouts by the fragments of their tubes cast upon the beach. I have seen large areas of these fragments out in the bay and used to wonder what they were. One could describe such an area as looking like a field of corn stubble, but each piece of "stubble" is the home of the sea worm, which, using the grains of sand as bricks, gradually builds a round tower, like a long, pliable factory chimney in miniature, around his delicate body.

Among the catches that the fishermen of Morecambe Bay bring home after trawling for shrimps can be found all kinds of creatures. Crabs, worms, clams, small plaice, soles and turbot, but among the innumerable fish that lie buried just below the surface of the sand with only their eyes showing are some that require very careful handling. Sandy bays often swarm with two curious little fishes, the dragonet and the weever whose local name is attapile. The dragonet has a three-sided blade knife set on either side of its head which can inflict painful cuts. The weever fish, though, is much worse, for the spines on its back and gill covers are hollow and connect with poisonous glands, like the fangs of a venomous snake. A sting from this fish can be extremely painful, and when a fisherman gets stung out in the bay miles from anywhere it is never easy to get immediate relief. An application of an alkali, such as ammonia or the dolly blue bag, is known to give relief but most fishermen I know have their own idea and urinate on the finger at the time of the sting.

Recently, because of my wide knowledge of the sands and the estuaries, I was invited to make up a party of three to walk across the Ribble estuary from Southport to Lytham St. Annes. At the start of the walk we were briefed by a lifeguard about the journey we were about to undertake. According to his calculations, we were going to be very lucky to make the journey without being stung by a weever fish or attackd by seagulls — he had told us of their behaviour to holiday-makers — or we would be in grave danger of quicksands. Furthermore he added, "You are bliddy fools for trying this and don't make a habit of it."

Well off we set from Southport Pier on sands that we, apart from the coastguard who accompanied us for part of the way, were strangers to. We reached our goal without coming across the dreaded weever fish or the crazy seagulls, and we must have avoided the treacherous quicksands, as we met coastguards from the other side in an inflatable as the Ribble was far too deep for us to ford. It was an experience I shall never forget, and which I believe we all enjoyed, but the dangers are always there for the unwary. The worst danger is always from the tide.